# The Prayer Request Of Christ

## And How You Can Be An Answer

*By: P. J. Meduri*

## *Unless otherwise noted:*

"Scripture quotations are from The Holy Bible, English Standard Version, copyright © 2001 by Crossway Bibles, a publishing ministry of Good News Publishers. Used by permission. All rights reserved." Scripture quotations marked NIV have been taken from the Holy Bible, New International Version. Copyright © 1973, 1978, 1984 by International Bible Society. Used by permission of Zondervan. All rights reserved. Scripture quotations marked HCSB have been taken from the Holman Christian Standard Bible, Copyright © 1999, 2000, 2002, 2003 by Holman Bible Publishers. Used by Permission. Holman Christian Standard Bible, Holman CSB, and HCSB are federally registered trademarks of Holman Bible Publishers. Scripture quotations marked NLT are taken from the Holy Bible, New Living Translation, copyright © 1996. Used by permission of Tyndale House Publishers, Inc., Wheaton, Illinois 60189. All rights reserved. Scripture quotations marked NKJV are taken from the New King James Version. Copyright © 1979, 1980, 1982 by Thomas Nelson Inc. Used by Permission. All rights reserved. When you quote various conversations you've been involved in over the years, or when you've heard comments from others, it's possible not to reproduce those word for word. However, quotes that appear in this book have been written so that each word is stated as best as memory permits and in no way changes the essence of what was shared in the slightest. It is the firm belief of the author that the sixty-six books that make up the Bible are the inspired, inerrant Word of God. They are "God-breathed." Therefore, whenever you read something in this work such as, "Paul writes," this is not to take away from the fact that the Holy Spirit is the real author of the Scriptures, using the writing abilities of men to communicate God's specific revelation to the human race. (2 Pet. 1:20-21) References to the Lord have been capitalized in what I wrote and in the Bible verses used. In some translations the words referring to the Lord were not capitalized, but have been done so in this work for the sake of continuity. Also any emphasis in the Bible verses used, whether they be underlined words or italics, have been placed there by the author to emphasize a certain point. Finally, there are times only a portion of a verse is used. Sometimes they are noted by ...at the beginning or the end of the verse; other times they are not. Format and readability were the determining factor in these situations.

## *All rights reserved.*

# Endorsements

A clear, practical, and biblically-based challenge to share the Good News of Jesus Christ--in both our home communities, and the farthest corners of the earth. PJ Meduri is a man who lives what he writes about. I strongly recommend this book to anyone seeking a deeper understanding of the motivations and practices that lead to effective, God-honoring evangelism!

*Joseph Anfuso, Founder and President, Forward Edge International*

I've known PJ Meduri since this concept of "compassion driven vision" for reaching the lost was being birthed in his heart. I've watched him pursue it and seen it blossom into the fruitful ministry he is now engaged in. He has modeled what he writes about in this book. Walk with him as you read it and let the fire of his "compassion driven vision" kindle a similar flame in your heart. Read the book again, passionately praying that God will open your eyes to the opportunity He has in mind for you to make a difference in someone's life. As you respond in obedience remember "It is God who works in you to will and to act according to his good purpose" (Philippians 2:13 NIV).

*Lud Golz, Pastor Emeritus Fellowship Bible Church; Chagrin Falls, Ohio, Radio Bible Teacher; "Getting God's Message"*

The heart of PJ for those who do not yet know Jesus as their Lord and Savior permeates the pages of "The Prayer Request of Christ." His emphasis on persevering prayers of compassion shows his heart is intertwined with that of the Father. PJ is a true evangelist who understands that the power of prayer through love is essential in bringing others to saving faith in Jesus Christ.

*Michael Gray, International Director/Pastor of Prayer and Evangelism Grace Extended Ministries International*

PJ Meduri challenges us to cooperate with what God is doing in the world in seeking and saving the lost. It's a challenge to be intentional and purposeful in changing our world through great prayers, great giving and great sacrifice, but in the end it results in great rewards. The 'Next Steps' section of the book is practical and a valuable resource for small group discussions.

*David L. Jones, Luis Palau Association*

This prayer of Jesus has become a calling to PJ from the day he accepted Jesus as his Savior. Through his personal life, the halls of academia, the sport fields and now Evangelism to a variety of countries throughout the world. This motivation to pray, to travel and now to write comes from his burning desire to follow the words of Jesus and to be sent out as a laborer into the harvest for Jesus. I highly recommend his writings to you, but more his lifestyle and work for the Lord.

*Paul Meduri, Pastor of Counseling; Venture Church, Streetsboro, Ohio*

What could be more important in doing God's will than being an answer to Jesus' very own call to prayer! My friend and ministry partner around the world, PJ has given this much thought, he's lived the life and been on the field of training and battle. Out of that experience he has now provided this helpful roadmap for disciples of Christ to live out their calling and win others to the Kingdom. I am stirred to KNOW the heart of Jesus more, I am stirred to GO in His name, PJ has challenged me to live out my calling right where I live and Be an Answer!

*~Andrew Palau, Evangelist*

Do you want to see people you know come to Jesus? Do you want to see God use your life to make a difference for eternity? If yes then this book is for you. PJ Meduri has written this powerful book with you in mind. I believe this book with give you the tools needed to have a tool chest ready to pray, plan, and prepare to be actively sharing your faith with others. This book will give you an inside look at the heart Jesus has for the lost and how you play an important part in the Great Commission. Get ready for this book to stir a fire in your heart for evangelism!

*Reid Saunders, Evangelist, Reid Saunders Association*

# Table of Contents

Acknowledgements .......................................................................... 7

Foreword ....................................................................................... 9

Introduction ................................................................................. 11

**Section One: Being An Answer Through Prayer**

Chapter One: A Prayer of Compassion ........................... 19

Chapter Two: Enlarging Our Hearts ............................... 33

Chapter Three: If You Pray, They Will Go ...................... 49

Chapter Four: Faith, Hope, and Love ............................. 63

**Section Two: Being An Answer Through Going**

Chapter Five: A Promised Partnership ............................ 81

Chapter Six: Just As ....................................................... 95

Chapter Seven: God So Loved The World ...................... 109

Chapter Eight: Taking The Step ..................................... 125

Chapter Nine: Finding Life ............................................ 133

Epilogue ....................................................................................... 151

Next Steps .................................................................................... 155

Additional Resources .................................................................. 164

Bibliography ................................................................................ 166

# Acknowledgements

When I look back over the last few years that this book has been in the "works," there have been so many people, places, projects, and personal experiences that have been integral to the final work. I'm grateful to all who have helped, even those who may not know that a word they spoke, an insight they shared, or a prayer they offered were used by God and impacted me on this journey. A few of these folks I'd like to note here.

First I'd like to thank my wife Delores for her love and faithfulness as my life partner. Without your support, prayers, encouragement, and many sacrifices, not only this book, but much of what's illustrated throughout its pages, would not have been possible. I love you more today than ever.

A lot of gratitude (and that's an understatement) goes to Lisa Vogt for her proofreading and editing of the manuscript. Lisa went "above and beyond"in her efforts and the Lord has truly gifted her in this area.

To Joanie, Jan, Lud, Mike, Wayne and Will, a much deserved thanks for being willing to read parts of, and in many cases all of, this manuscript. I appreciate and thank you for your time, encouragement, and insights on this project and sharing the words that motivated me to complete the work.

Thanks very much to Jim Hale for his work on this project and on many of the materials that our ministry has been using the last couple of years. The seed is being sown internationally through your ministry.

I'm grateful to my friends who provided testimonies in Chapter Eight and my various friends and colleagues who wrote an endorsement. What you've all modeled in "Being an Answer" has been used by God to inspire me in many ways. And to Dr. Tim Robnett for not only writing the Foreword but for being a mentor to me in the ministry – Dr. Tim, without your insights and support along the way, many of the stories in this book would not be there.

Thanks also to our board members past and present. Without each of you, Taking the Field Ministries would never have been possible.

I also want to recognize my mentor, Dr. Bill Thomas. In July of 2014, The Lord decided it was time to bring Dr. Bill home to glory. I'm so glad that I was able to serve with him and learn over a six-year period before his illness began to slow him down. Dr. Bill, your legacy continues through so many like myself. I look forward to seeing you again someday. Thanks for all you did for so many like me. Therefore, it is my honor to share this work in your memory.

A heartfelt thank you to Pete and Doris Meduri, my parents. What an honor for me to call you Dad and Mom. Thanks for being great parents. I love you both very much.

And last but not least to Walter and June Hedgecock, my in-laws. Shortly before this book went to print, Walter was called home to be with the Lord at age 92. I'm thankful to Walter and to June for their prayers and encouragement for close to thirty years.

# Foreword

Armchair quarterbacks give opinions on a weekly basis, touching hundreds of games each week during the football season. It is far easier to observe and make comments, whether good or bad, than to participate in the demanding sport of football at whatever level of competition. In our Christian journey we can be susceptible to the same mindset and lifestyle. *The Prayer Request of Christ* calls us to experience the heart of Jesus in a personal and practical way. PJ Meduri outlines for those desiring to make a difference for Jesus Christ to step up to the challenge of being an answer instead of seeking an answer.

PJ is one who lives the Christian life with all seriousness and joy. He has become an example to many of what it means to truly follow Christ and invite others to join in that journey. PJ did not arrive at this level of effective Christian living by accident. He discovered that Jesus Christ has clear teaching and training for those who truly want to follow the Master. Our Lord came to seek and save those who are lost. He calls and inspires all who hear His voice to do the same. *The Prayer Request of Christ* outlines the mandate of a life of prayer and evangelism. Prayer becomes the fire that ignites our hearts to make a difference, to go where we have not gone before, to become what we are not, to believe the Lord will use us to help others discover the most important relationship of life and eternity.

We do need to seek God for the answers to many personal and family challenges. But *The Prayer Request of Christ* suggests that God has something bigger and better in mind for each of those who will follow His lead.

To "Be An Answer" means that I will be a doer of God's Word by embracing a new level of prayer, evangelistic prayers and praise, and in praising God for who He is and what He has done. *The Prayer Request of Christ* introduces one to a lifestyle of engaging with people about the deepest issues of life, the issue of one's relationship with God. Prayer is the key that unleashes the Christian to a greater level of communicating the Gospel.

The book becomes a practical guide into how to develop a powerful personal life of prayer and evangelism. As one who is journeying with PJ, I can add to his challenge that prayer truly does empower us in being the witnesses the Lord has designed us to be. It is the most fulfilling life, not just in a selfish way, but in the way of transformation of others. Seeing and experiencing the joy of people liberated from their stresses, frustrations, and fears into a life with God cannot be compared to any other human experience. To be used of God to introduce someone to Jesus Christ is truly a joy incomparable. *The Prayer Request of Christ* will introduce you into a new dimension of seeing God at work within and through you.

Dr. Timothy Robnett
President, Tim Robnett Ministries
North Plains, Oregon
Adjunct Professor, Multnomah Seminary
Portland, Oregon

# Introduction

Eight years ago, my wife and I sold our home in Northeast Ohio and moved to West Virginia, where Delores was raised. Since we'd been married for twenty years, I had traveled to this state numerous times to visit her family. Early in our marriage, during one of our visits to the state that the late musician John Denver labeled "Almost Heaven," I was introduced to some outdoor recreation known as baling hay. Now if you've never had the privilege of spending an afternoon picking up these rectangular bundles of prickly straw, this might be a good time to put the book down and offer a prayer of thanks. The work is hot and heavy, and if you don't grow weary picking up the bales in the field, then stacking them in the barn is the perfect time to fake an injury. At times I wonder if the work isn't part farming and part prayer meeting, since you tend to hear the words "have mercy" quite often after you reach bale number twenty.

One summer on an early Saturday night, after we had moved, I was preparing to relax and review my speaking outline for a church service the following morning. Since it was a nice evening, I thought I might sit outside. That's when I looked to the hills on my left and saw my brother-in-law. He was walking in the field, picking up the hay he'd just baled and loading the bales onto the wagon behind his tractor ...all by himself. At this point the mental battle began. Should I help him, or should I change plans and go back inside to review? After all, I did have to speak the following morning, which seemed like a valid excuse to let him finish his task alone. Then to my mind came the verse… "Do to others what you would have them to do to you." (Matt. 7:12, NIV) After a thought like that, it was going to be difficult to head back inside the house with any kind of peace. I certainly tried, but failed in my attempt to rationalize why I shouldn't go and help him. So reluctantly I changed clothes, grabbed a pair of gloves and decided to go and attend this outdoor prayer meeting. "Have mercy!"

At times I wasn't sure we would ever finish. As I stood on the tractor, tossing the bales into the barn for Steve to stack, it seemed like every time I tossed one off, two more appeared. I started thinking, "Lord, I really believe that when that little boy brought you his lunch that day, the bread and fish his mom had packed for him that morning, I really believe you took it and turned it into a meal for thousands with lots of leftovers for later. I believe it, I have no doubts, I'm not a skeptic, so you really don't have to do it again by multiplying these bales of hay."

Finally we finished, and as I was walking back to my house, I wondered if my brother-in-law had prayed for someone to come and help him with the work. My thoughts were the result of an illustration I'd read many years earlier in the handbook, "Share Jesus Without Fear," by Bill Fay and Ralph Hodge. It's a story of a farmer who was afraid that it would rain on the hay that he'd just cut. This story connected the words of Jesus, asking us to pray for an increase in workers for His harvest, with baling hay.

> The farmer told me his son was in a truck heading for town. Migrant workers and others seeking hourly work gathered there on a particular corner to be available for area farmers who needed temporary laborers. Trucks usually came by early in the morning and chose the number of workers needed for the day, loaded them up, and took them to the fields. But since it was afternoon, he feared that the workers would have already given up on work for the day and gone home.

> I'll never forget the desperation in the faithful Christian farmer's voice. He asked me, "Please pray that there will be workers at the corner, and enough to help me get my hay up before it rains."

> The prayer request wasn't for the hay in the fields. The hay

wasn't going anywhere. He didn't appeal for prayer so that the rain wouldn't come. His hope was to find enough workers he could depend on to do what needed to be done.

While praying for the lost, I have often heard that farmer's voice appealing to God for enough workers. At the same time I also hear Jesus' voice as He asks us to pray for people willing to go to the lost and tell them how to be saved. [1]

The plea from the farmer in that excerpt is indeed the plea of Jesus in relation to a different harvest. A harvest of souls. And with a world growing larger by the day, this prayer request of Christ is needing an answer as much today as it ever has. Will you be that answer?

## FIRST THINGS FIRST

Sadly, there seems to be a lot of negativity toward the church today. We'd all agree there's no perfect church, but we might be better served if we would exercise caution in bashing something that Christ is the head of and loves. At the same time, as followers of Christ, it's time to realize we may have been neglecting what could arguably be one of the most important prayers recorded in the Bible. It's a request from Christ, who's asking and expecting us to pray for Him to send more workers into the world. Jesus said, "But seek first the kingdom of God and His righteousness." (Matt. 6:33) Praying for Christ to send workers into His harvest would truly fall into that category. It's also a way we can make a revolutionary change in our prayer life, and the prayer life of our church. It's a way we can all participate in advancing the Kingdom of God. In doing so, we can become an answer to Christ's request.

## IS THIS REALLY A REQUEST?

When you hear the phrase "the prayer request of Christ," what comes to mind? A couple of people I've spoken with immediately thought of the great prayer that Jesus prayed prior to His arrest and crucifixion. This insightful and inspiring prayer is recorded in John Chapter 17. In that chapter Jesus makes many requests to His Father: requests for Himself, requests for His disciples, and requests for all of His followers throughout history. However, in Matthew 9 and Luke 10, Jesus isn't making a request of His Father; He's making a request of us. In those Scriptures, instead of praying for Himself and His followers, He's asking His followers to pray for something very important to Him.

Picture sitting in a prayer meeting and Jesus is there …. bodily. When the pastor or leader of the service asks if anyone has any requests, anything that they'd like others to pray about, the room suddenly grows silent. Jesus has just raised His hand. Those who weren't prepared to write down the requests, quickly begin searching their pockets for a pen, or power up their smartphones to access the notes page. No one wants to miss this request. And, with all attention riveted on Jesus, He finally speaks, saying: "Pray for Me to send more workers into My harvest field!" That's His request. One that He's given to me. And one that He's given to you.

One of the English definitions for the word request is *"an act of politely or formally asking for something."*[2] But in the Biblical context it's a whole lot stronger. One of the Greek words associated with the word request is "deomai," and it's used as a word for prayer that's defined with a variety of terms such as, want, need, beg, request, beseech and pray. It's also described as, *"to feel a pressing need because of lack"* and *"to make an urgent appeal."*[3] If we look at how Matthew records these words from Jesus, then the request is actually framed as a command – something the Lord expects from His followers. So why call it a request?

I admit, I've struggled with this. I certainly don't want to water things down, or change what's actually being taught in the Scriptures. And I definitely don't want to minimize the importance of the Lord's plea, nor to portray a false premise that this is a choice a disciple can either make or forego. This isn't any more of an option or suggestion than sexual purity is for a Christ-follower. By using the word "request," I am hoping to communicate that the Lord is not making an appeal for us to pray and go based solely on His right to do so as Lord. That alone should be enough. But by using the word "request," I hope it presents the personal side to this prayer. To present the way this prayer flowed from the heart of Jesus. A personal and deeply felt need of the Savior, that resulted in this call to pray. And that by grasping the heart of the Lord in relation to this prayer, our hearts will be touched as well, creating within us the desire to obey and live as an answer to His great and compassionate request. In doing so, you and I, and our churches as a whole, have an opportunity to touch people and places in this world in ways beyond anything we can imagine. Places and people who right now live in hopeless darkness, but will soon hear of Christ, because of a process that begins with your prayers.

By praying for Christ to send workers, we become an answer to His request. But to be a complete answer, it will also involve going. To be one of the answers we're praying for. In Section One of this book, we'll focus on being an answer through prayer, though brief comments will also be made in relation to going as well. In Section Two we'll focus on going. Whether it's going across the street, or across the world, each of us has a role in the fields that Christ said "are white for harvest." (John 4:35) In doing so, I pray that the Lord will not only encourage you with the role He's given you at home, but also enlarge your vision for people and places far away. Both of these may look different for each of us, but in Section Two we'll look at how the Lord has not only "sent" each of us, He's also placed a world perspective in our hearts as well – one that He wants to unleash in some way. So I pray that you'll approach that section and its corresponding chapters with anticipation. There are some new, God-ordained desires and opportunities waiting to emerge in your heart and life.

## COME UP HERE

A pastor once reminded me that when people hear the word of God, they often feel like they're being beaten down, that they are filtering what's being said through the lens of how they're failing. That's not the goal of this book. These pages aren't an attempt to push the failure button, or the guilt switch. Instead they're designed to push the button of truth in love, so we'll begin seeing all of our lives in relation to what God is really saying. Failure and/or guilt is not the goal or intention. However, if this book convicts, that's good, since conviction is the role of the Holy Spirit and not the author. If you sense conviction as you read, don't run from it, run to it. Conviction is actually a beautiful thing; it is God's way of showing us that we're not yet where He wants to take us. Therefore, instead of a "push down," it is an invitation and an opportunity to come up to a higher level of understanding and intimacy in our relationship with Christ – an opportunity to "grow in the grace and knowledge of our Lord and Savior Jesus Christ." (2 Pet. 3:18) Something only He can bring about, and something He wants to see happen. The Bible says, "He who calls you is faithful; He will surely do it." (1 Thess. 5:24) Our role is to cooperate with what He's doing in our lives and respond to the sense of conviction, that He loves us enough to give. And in doing so, we will open our hearts and lives for Him to do in and through us what He's seeking to do.

## GETTING AWAY WITH JESUS

When Jesus sent the twelve apostles on their first mission, Luke records what happened upon their return. "On their return the apostles told Him all that they had done. And He took them and withdrew apart to a town called Bethsaida." (Luke 9:10) I'm sure this was more than just a time of rest, but a time to review and learn from all that they had experienced. With this in mind, each chapter will end with a time for reflection called "Getting Away with Jesus." This is an opportunity to review the chapter, any key notes you may have made, or reflect on the questions and/or activities that are provided. Allow the Lord to speak to you about Himself and His desire for you in relation to what you've just read. Are there one or two things that really resonated with you, convicted you, or inspired you to pursue further?

As you look at how the Lord is leading you to begin living as an answer, my counsel would be to think of the word "Next." What is the next step or steps the Lord is leading you to take? I remember the words of a speaker I heard while I was still in public education. She said, "What one thing will you do as a result of what you've heard today?" That's my prayer for you as you "Get Away With Jesus" and reflect on each chapter. In doing so, if you begin to feel a little overwhelmed, take a deep breath and prioritize things. Some things will coincide while others will be separate. Some you'll easily be able to begin making a part of your life. Others may take time. The Lord is going to take each of us through the race marked out for us, one step at a time. The questions and thoughts at the end of each chapter are meant to help you spend time with the Lord and see that next step.

To help with the next step, in the back of the book there's a section titled, "Next Steps." Here you'll find ideas and resources to help you, your family, your church, or your small group to live out some of the principles and ideas, by taking that next step in the power of the Holy Spirit. I hope that what you find will be helpful as is, or help stimulate other similar ideas that will be of assistance.

As we get ready to begin, I pray that the essence of this journey will result in a greater desire to know and seek Christ. That's the ultimate and I hope, the theme that will consistently emerge through these chapters. And as a result, may the natural outflow of our growing relationship with the King of kings, and Lord of lords, be one where you and I, as well as our churches, will become ongoing answers to Christ's request. A complete answer: an answer that prays, and an answer that goes. And that being an answer will become a normal part of our life in Christ. May God bless you and may you be a blessing to Him, and to others.

# Section One

# Being an
# Answer
# Through Prayer

*"A person who can pray is the mightiest instrument Christ has in this world. A praying church is stronger than the gates of hell."* E.M. Bounds [1]

# 1
# A Prayer Of Compassion

Perhaps the name Bob Pierce is not a familiar one. Though he may or may not be well known, many Christians will probably recognize one of the two ministries he helped found. The first is World Vision and the second is Samaritan's Purse, now led by Franklin Graham. The latter ministry is one you may have even participated in through a program called Operation Christmas Child. In 1990 a couple from Wales were moved by a television broadcast depicting Romanian orphanages. Wanting to do something to help, Dave and Jill Cooke loaded nine trucks with various items including Christmas gifts and took them to Romania. In 1993 the idea was adopted by Franklin Graham and Samaritan's Purse.[1] Today, only two decades later, each Christmas numerous churches and individuals pack shoe boxes with toys, clothes, school supplies and other necessities so that a poor child in another nation can receive a Christmas gift. Both World Vision and Samaritan's Purse continue making an enormous impact in lives around the world and each can be traced back to one man's burden to make a difference … Bob Pierce. A burden that may have emerged from a simple, yet powerful prayer that Pierce prayed many years earlier.

After World War II, Pierce made an evangelistic trip to China where God touched his heart with the widespread hunger he saw in that nation. Later he would write the following words in his Bible: "Let my heart be broken with the things that break the heart of God."[2] Judging by Pierce's life, and the organizations he founded, it appears that God did indeed answer his prayer. Pastor Richard Halverson wrote that Pierce *"prayed more earnestly and importunely than anyone else I have ever known. It was as though prayer burned within him ... Bob Pierce functioned from a broken heart."*[3] Which is exactly what he prayed for.

This brings us to a question based on the prayer Pierce prayed decades ago. What is it that actually breaks the heart of God?

To answer that question will require a lot of time and a lot of space. Perhaps more space than the world's largest computer can hold. Then, after wearing out our keypads with endless lists causing this computer to crash, we'd still just be scratching the surface in compiling answers. Since God is infinite and we're not, an exhaustive answer to the question, "what breaks the heart of God" can't be known entirely in this lifetime. That doesn't mean we're left completely in the dark, though. The Bible, especially the life of Jesus as revealed in the gospels, provides quite a bit of light. And to help shine a light on the heartbreak of Christ, the gospel writers employ the word "compassion" to help us understand. To prepare us for the New Testament definition for compassion, we'll begin by looking at the term in English.

## MORE THAN A FEELING

In 1976 the band "Boston" released a hit single titled "More Than A Feeling." Close to 40 years later it's still recognized as one of the best rock songs of all time. Though the title (and the song) isn't about compassion, it does reflect the way true compassion is defined. Compassion is a term that represents more than a feeling, but a feeling leading to action. The English word for compassion is a *"sympathetic consciousness of others' distress, together with a desire to alleviate it."*[4]

Looking at the second part of the definition, we see that although compassion begins with a feeling, it isn't designed to end there. It puts us on a path toward some type of action to help make a difference. This is what Bob Pierce did when his heart was broken, and it's what the Cookes did when they saw the distress of the Romanian orphans. It's also what countless others have done throughout history in a variety of ways. Individuals, churches, and organizations that weren't content to just "feel" compassion; they had a desire that led to action. This really shouldn't surprise us, since this is the example Jesus set. Time and time again the gospels reveal how Jesus took action in alleviating distresses that people experienced.

While Jesus walked the earth He literally touched people in their distress. He didn't just "feel," nor did He act from a distance. He entered homes, He gave of His time, and He put His hands on those whom many believed to be "untouchable." He had a definite "hands-on" minstry.

Ultimately this would take Him all the way to the cross and the greatest act of compassion in all of human history: an act that would make it possible for our greatest distress, separation from God, to be alleviated.

That's a brief look at the English definition of compassion. Now let's turn our attention to the way this word is used in the New Testament – to the way the gospel writers define it. In doing so, we'll gain a deeper understanding of the heartbreak of Christ and the way He responded as a result.

## A G-RATED DEFINITION

The Holy Spirit inspired four men – Matthew, Mark, Luke and John – to serve as biographers for the earthly life of Jesus. They inform us of many things, including the emotional moments Jesus experienced as He encountered the distress of people. To describe some of these heartbreaking moments, three of the the four writers, Matthew, Mark and Luke, often utilize the Greek word **splanchnizomai.** It's a word for compassion and depicts someone who had an extremely strong emotional reaction.

This new G-rated, or Greek definition for compassion employed by the writers means, *"To be moved as to one's bowels, hence to be moved with compassion, have compassion (for the bowels were thought to be the seat of love and pity)."*[5] In commenting on this, Pastor John MacArthur wrote the following:

> ...The Hebrews, like many other ancient peoples, expressed attitudes and emotions in terms of physiological symptoms, not in abstractions ...The heart was the source of thought and action, whereas the bowels were the responder, the reactor. Jesus therefore used the common term of His day to express his deep compassion for the great crowds of people who were suffering. But His care was not merely figurative, because He felt in His own body the symptoms of His deep caring. If our bodies literally ache in pain and nausea when we

experience great agony, remorse or sympathy, we can be sure that the Son of Man felt even more.[6]

To move from the world of definitions to reality, let's put it like this. Have you ever had an agonizing experience that caused you not only emotional but physical pain, a feeling like being "punched in the gut?" If so, then you've had a taste of what Jesus felt. It is this type of compassion, this deep-seated, heartbreaking emotional and physical pain, that prompted Jesus to respond, usually with a miracle.

One of these miracles was a closeup encounter with two blind men who cried out, "Lord … open our eyes." Moved with **compassion**, Jesus touched their eyes. "Immediately they could see, and they followed Him." (Matt. 20:33-34, HCSB) Another time Jesus said, "I have **compassion** on the crowd, because they've already stayed with Me three days and have nothing to eat. If I send them home famished, they will collapse on the way, and some of them have come a long distance." (Mark 8:23, HCSB) Shortly thereafter, seven loaves and a few fish miraculously turned into a meal for 4,000-plus people … with leftovers. Once again we see the Messianic equation emerge. Suffering + Compassion = A Miracle.

As moving as these first two scriptural examples are, once news of the following account spread around town, it would have been hard to find a dry eye for blocks. Had Youtube been around two thousand years ago, this is one of those videos that would have gone viral …. instantly.

> Just as He neared the gate of the town, a dead man was being carried out. He was his mother's only son and she was a widow. A large crowd from the city was also with her. When the Lord saw her, He had **compassion** on her and said, "Don't cry." Then He came up and touched the open coffin, and the pallbearers stopped. And He said, "Young man, I tell you get up!" The dead man sat up and began to speak, and Jesus gave him to his mother. (Luke 7:12-15, HCSB)

From the blind and lame, to the sick and afflicted, to the hungry masses and those in mourning, the compassion of Christ usually led to a miracle. Usually. But not on that particular day in Galilee recorded by Matthew.* A time when Jesus was hurting, and agonizing over the circumstances of people, but this time it wasn't due to a physical need. It wasn't sympathy

*In Mark 6:34 Jesus also felt compassion for the people because they were sheep without a shepherd and responded by teaching them.

over those who mourned. This time, His heartbreak involved the condition of souls. And this time, instead of a miracle, His response was surprisingly different and probably unexpected. Yet this unexpected response has influenced people like Bob Pierce and many others for two thousand years. This time, instead of a miracle, Jesus responded by making an appeal for prayer. The ex-tax collector turned Apostle, turned gospel writer Matthew, helps set the stage for this unique and unexpected response.

## THE HEART OF THE MATTER

For three and a half years, Jesus and miracles were synonymous. The gospel of Matthew is one place where we catch a glimpse of the Lord's very busy "miracle tour." Beginning in Chapter Eight, Matthew records the story of Jesus healing a leper. By the time we near the end of Chapter Nine, Matthew describes eight more specific miracles, all in less than two chapters. Then as if to put an exclamation point on all that Jesus was doing, Matthew wrote the following:

> And Jesus went throughout all the cities and villages, teaching in their synagogues and proclaiming the gospel of the kingdom and healing every disease and every affliction.
>
> (Matt. 9:35)

To record the word "all" regarding cities and villages, and "every" in regard to diseases and illnesses, indicates the enormous impact that Jesus was having on lives in that region. And it was amid this busy teaching and "hands-on-miracle-working" schedule that Matthew pulls out his pen and describes the "gut-wrenching" compassion experienced by Jesus:

> When He saw the crowds, He had compassion for them, because they were harassed and helpless, like sheep without a shepherd. (Matt. 9:36)

Matthew doesn't share the exact way Jesus displayed His compassion. He doesn't say whether Jesus shed tears, hung His head, or sighed and uttered words like "I'm really hurting for these people!" Whatever took place to reveal Jesus' feelings, it must have been noticeable, for Matthew to use the word **splanchnizomai**. This time, however, the reason for the hurt in Jesus' heart wasn't in regard to crippling physical diseases, but due to a crippling spiritual one. Now His "bowel-breaking" compassion wasn't due to blind eyes, but blind hearts. Now His agony emerged from the spiritual condition of people's souls.

The metaphor Jesus used to describe the people was "sheep without a Shepherd." If you lived at this time and heard those words you would know that to be an actual four-legged sheep and survive without the guidance and care of a shepherd was impossible. You would be living in a hopeless, helpless state where danger was imminent. The picture is clear. Apart from Christ, people are also living in a state of grave danger spiritually. Regardless of whether people were (and are today) healthy or sick, rich or poor, young or old, they were lacking the spiritual guidance and understanding necessary to put them in a right relationship with God.

One reason the people of Jesus' time were living life as "sheep without a Shepherd" was due to the false and burdensome teachings they received from the present day religious leaders. Jesus accurately accused them: "So for the sake of your tradition you have made void the word of God." (Matt. 15:6) He later said, "They crush you with impossible religious demands and never lift a finger to help ease the burden." (Matthew 23:4, NLT) Because of this lack of spiritual guidance and man-centered traditions, people were harassed (faint), and helpless. They were in a state of spiritual desperation. They needed someone who could bring them hope. They needed someone who could point them to the ultimate Shepherd, Jesus Himself, (1 Pet. 2:25), someone who could give "rest to their souls". (Matt 11:29) Until that happened, the hearts of the people would feel hopeless and heavy, resulting in a variety of consequences both now and in eternity. I received a glimpse of some of these consequences one day on a ministry trip to Eastern Europe. When I did, it gripped my heart as well.

## COMPASSION IN THE PARK

The park was large and the surrounding apartments showed signs of wear and tear. Age, and a few overlooked repairs had downgraded some of the living conditions for many in the area.

Though the grass was green and seemed to be well kept, a used syringe was also spotted lying on the ground, left behind by one of the local addicts. Our team of four was in the Ukraine working with local churches on an evangelistic outreach. Two days of public meetings were to be held in this park, an area that was home to many distressed people, including alcoholics, drug addicts and prostitutes.

As I waited to take the stage and share the gospel, I was moved with compassion over the hopeless condition of many in that area. When people are living apart from Christ, the Shepherd of their souls, devastating things can happen. Christ knows the tragedy of this and it breaks His heart.

He knows that living apart from Him can result in problems that not only ruin individuals, but have a ripple effect on others as well. That day in the Ukraine the death, destruction, and ruination caused by sin was on display and I too began to function from a broken heart.

The Bible states over and over that Jesus gives us eternal life, saving us from the coming wrath of Almighty God. But eternal life is a present reality as well, making a difference in our lives here and now. Jesus not only saves people from eternal destruction, He also saves people from the things that ruin our lives during our time on earth. Paul wrote in Galatians, "Grace to you and peace from God our Father and the Lord Jesus Christ, who gave Himself for our sins to deliver us from the present evil age, according to the will of our God and Father." (Gal. 1:3-4)

That day, as I took the stage and began to speak, the impact of this present evil age that was destroying so many in that area filled me with compassion. A compassion that can be traced right to the heart of Christ and the new heart He placed in me the day I was "born again" (more about this new heart in Chapter Two). This "new heart" was the same one Christ placed in Bob Pierce, inspiring him to begin World Vision and Samaritan's Purse. It's this new heart that has sent many believers for two thousand years to share the love of Christ in word and deed to people around the world. And it's this new heart that beats inside of you as a follower of Christ, ready to take you out of your comfort zone in order to be a part of His harvest field. That day in the Ukraine, the new heart that had taken me there in the first place was beating rapidly for those standing in the park. Some held beer bottles, some heckled, but all were in need of a Shepherd.

The Bible verse that came to mind before I began to speak was the one in which Jesus shared the sharp contrast between life with Him and life without Him. "The thief (Satan) comes only to steal and kill and destroy. I (Jesus) came that they may have life and have it abundantly." (John 10:10) As I took the platform and began to share that verse my voice starting cracking as I said, "It's time to say 'no more', to this thief," who was stealing, killing and destroying so many lives, and so many eternities.

I finished my message and walked off the stage to the place where our team was standing. A break was scheduled so that people could go and have their dinner, but I decided to stay in the park to prepare for the evening meeting. A night that led to the ultimate reality of why it was that Jesus is broken over people without Him.

## COMPLETE COMPASSION

Before we return to that evening in the park, I'd like to take a moment and address something I'm going to call "complete compassion." Without question the heart of Jesus breaks over many things. We mentioned some in an earlier section regarding the miracles Jesus performed. These miracles not only revealed that Jesus is Lord and God just as He says, but it also showed people how He genuinely cares. He cares about the details of our lives. He cares about the hurts, the sicknesses, the evils, the injustices and all of the things that this sin-cursed world has brought about. A world that wasn't His intention when He first created it, and one that He'll redeem and restore to its intended perfection in His future Kingdom. In the meantime, as followers of Christ, we're commanded to make a difference in the world and for people in various ways. There's certainly no shortage of temporal, social, physical needs and injustices for you and I to help address. When we do, we help bring a redemptive element to all parts of society, showing our love for God and our love for others with the ultimate goal of God receiving the glory. (Matt. 5:16, 1 Pet. 2:12)

However, if we stop at good works and neglect to share the good news, we're not really helping injustice. In fact, we're actually perpetuating the biggest injustice of all: an injustice against those we're only partially helping, and an injustice against Christ, who gave His life to spare us from the coming judgment. Jonathan Martin in his book Giving Wisely, asks, "What kind of Christian would I be to feed someone their whole life long and yet never present the gospel to him? Keep them alive so they simply could experience an eternal death away from the presence of their Creator?"[7]

While it's true that Jesus rescues people from this present evil age and from the destruction that the wages of sin bring into this world, it's also of the utmost importance to understand one of the meanings behind the term "harvest." Though Jesus is Lord of the harvest occurring this very moment, He's also Lord over the harvest as it relates to the coming judgment. Here are two passages relating to this.

> The field is the world, and the good seed is the sons of the kingdom. The weeds are the sons of the evil one, and the enemy who sowed them is the devil. The **harvest** is the close of the age, and the reapers are angels. Just as the weeds are gathered and burned with fire, so will it be at the close of the age. The Son of Man will send His angels, and they will gather out of His kingdom all causes of sin and all law-breakers, and throw them into the fiery furnace. In that place there will be weeping and gnashing of teeth. Then the righteous will shine like the sun in the kingdom of their Father. He who has ears, let him hear. (Matt. 13:38-43)

> And he (an angel) said with a loud voice, "Fear God and give Him glory, because the hour of His judgment has come, and worship Him who made heaven and earth, the sea and the springs of water.".....Then I looked, and behold, a white cloud, and seated on the cloud one like a Son of Man, with a golden crown on His head, and a sharp sickle in His hand. And another angel came out of the temple, calling with a loud voice to Him who sat on the cloud, "Put in your sickle, and reap, for the hour to reap has come for the **harvest** is fully ripe." So He who sat on the cloud swung his sickle across the earth, and the earth was reaped. (Rev. 14:7, 14-16)

These passages (see also Rev. 14:17-20) equate the harvest with a future judgment and help us realize why Jesus was brokenhearted over the people He saw. Jesus wept over Jerusalem because they had rejected Him. (Luke 19:40-41) They were happy to receive His healing, but turned their backs on Him as the Messiah. As a result, Christ wept. The Lord also said, "Have I any pleasure in the death of the wicked, declares the Lord GOD, and not rather that he should turn from his way and live?" (Ezekiel 18:23)

The holiness of God demands a payment for sin, so a day of judgment is coming and it will not be overlooked. The love and compassion of God caused Him to send His son to pay the price and take the judgment that was rightfully ours. However, if people reject so great a salvation, there's nothing left "but a fearful expectation of judgment." (Heb. 10:27) That's ultimately why the Lord has such compassion over people who are sheep without a Shepherd. Without a doubt, He's concerned about every aspect of life. And yes, we're to bring a redemptive kingdom element into every part of our culture. But if we fail to understand that the greatest need of everyone – to be reconciled with God – then instead of bringing complete compassion, we're actually living and serving with incomplete compassion. This is not true Christ-based compassion – the type of compassion He felt that day when He looked on the masses in Galilee. I've been reminded of the reality and need of "complete compassion" many times in my walk with Christ. This trip to the Ukraine would remind me once again.

## A MEETING WITH THE SHEPHERD

As people began returning from dinner for the evening service in the Ukrainian park, I was unaware of something that had taken place that afternoon. Later I learned of a woman who was part of the worship team for the outreach and had given a testimony on how she became a follower of Jesus. The woman happened to be HIV-positive, a result of some of the consequences of her life before Christ. But now as a follower of Jesus, she was on the stage leading worship and telling the story of what Christ had done in her life. As she was sharing, she looked into the crowd and noticed an alcoholic by the name of "Victor." When she did, she stopped and said, "Victor, I recognize you; you were in that hospital I was in six years ago. Victor, you need to get right with God."

That night after proclaiming the gospel, I invited people to respond to Christ in repentance and faith. The first man who made his way toward our stage was having difficulty walking. I learned later that it was Victor, the alcoholic whom the worship leader had challenged during our afternoon meeting.

One of the churches involved in the outreach operated a rehabilitation center for recovering addicts. Many of the men who lived at the center immediately came to the front, surrounded Victor, and began ministering to him. It was a powerful picture of the family of Christ in action working together. Eventually these men helped to carry Victor away and they took him to the "rehab" center where they lived, and where our team was also staying that week in the Ukraine.

This all occurred on a Wednesday night. Friday morning as I came down the wooden steps to the open room where we would be having breakfast, the man who was organizing our week of ministry said, "PJ, go get your passport, the police are coming." Since I normally carry my passport, I was able to stay in the breakfast area and await the arrival of the police. While waiting I learned why the police were coming to the center. Victor had died in his sleep.

Approximately 30 hours earlier he had placed his trust in Christ. After being taken to the rehab center he spent the following day with the men who lived there, reading the Bible and praying with them. Then on Thursday evening, Victor went to sleep and woke up with Jesus in paradise.

I'm so grateful that Christ saves us from the present evil age. History is filled with stories of individual lives and families that have been saved from pain, ruin, and destruction due to the limitless power of Jesus Christ. But the ultimate reason for helping people to find the one and only Shepherd was a vivid reality that day in Eastern Europe, the day a rescued alcoholic named Victor went to be with Jesus, the Shepherd of his soul. The Shepherd who not only shared the reason for His broken-hearted compassion two thousand years ago in Galilee – but the Shepherd who also shared His solution to the problem that caused His heart to break in the first place.

## AN UNEXPECTED RESPONSE

When you combine massive numbers of people, harassed and helpless and looking for hope with very few people showing them where to find it, the result is a brokenhearted Christ. And from this broken heart Matthew sets the stage for the Lord to respond in an unexpected way. This time, instead of a miracle, Jesus did something different. In fact He didn't actually "do" anything. Instead He said something and what He said became one of the most important statements in the entire Bible.

> Then He said to His disciples, "The harvest is plentiful, but the laborers are few; therefore pray earnestly to the Lord of the harvest to send out laborers into His harvest."
> (Matthew 9:37-38)

Surprised? If so, try to put yourself in the position of the disciples at that time. Is this what you'd expect from someone who was visibly and verbally broken over the people's condition? Especially when the compassion of Christ usually led to healings and other supernatural acts. But this time there would be no miracle. No healing, no feeding, no casting out of a demon, or restoring the life of the dead. This time the broken heart of Christ pointed us toward prayer. And since this prayer was motivated from the heart of Christ, we can label it a prayer of compassion. A prayer He wants us to hear, but most of all a prayer He's expecting us to pray. And though His response might appear unusual at first, it's His perfect will and plan for meeting humankind's greatest need. The need for eternal life. The need for reconciliation with God.

Jesus was broken over the soul-condition of young and old and also over the supply-and-demand problem that was evident. He recognized that the supply of workers fell far below what was needed for the work. In response, the initial step that Christ designed to narrow that gap, a gap two thousand years ago, as well as the gap existing today, is prayer. A prayer of compassion.

Today as Jesus looks upon the world, He sees even greater numbers of people. People like the ones I saw in the Ukrainian park. People like you and me before we met Christ. People living across the street and around the world who need to be reconciled with God. Some are happy, successful, upstanding citizens. They're nice, friendly, and contribute to their communities, yet they're sheep without a Shepherd and dead in their sins. The heart of Jesus aches for them. A worker is needed.

Others are involved in destructive behaviors that hurt themselves and the people around them. The heart of Jesus aches for them too. And workers are needed. Regardless of outward appearances, the Lord sees each heart and understands a person's real condition. So He's looking for people. People who will understand His heart and the need for more workers and who will pray. People who will not only obey by being an answer through prayer, but who will obey by going as well. The prayer of compassion leads to the most needed miracle of all: the need for people who can go into all the world and show others how to find the Good Shepherd.

## THE BEAT OF YOUR HEART

As we looked at some definitions for compassion, one thing is clear. It's a deep emotion that results in action. It goes beyond sentiment, pity, and empathy. It transitions from having a feeling, to knowing how one feels, to actually trying to help in some way. This is what Bob Pierce did, because this is what Jesus did. It's also a part of the prayer of compassion.

As Jesus requests His followers to pray for workers, He also expects us to enter into the suffering of countless sheep living without the Shepherd.

Think about some of the things that tug at your heart. Things that bring a sense of compassion from deep within you. Perhaps it's the pictures of a starving child, or thoughts of people who live alone, especially during the holidays. Maybe it's the grief-stricken at funerals, or the helpless condition of many elderly, or a hospital patient who is terminally ill. Perhaps you're in the business world, and surrounded by people who are very successful and appear to have it "all together." Yet you know differently, because you too were like that once, and you want them to find Jesus just like you did.

If you're a follower of Jesus, you have a new heart in you. When God gives us a heart for someone, take notice. I believe we're experiencing a piece of His heart breaking within us, the new heart and new spirit He gave us when we trusted Him as our Lord and Savior. And if I were a betting man, I'd bet on the fact that the reason God is allowing this heartbreak in your life is because there's so much to do and a worker is needed to enter this suffering so that someone can find the Shepherd.

By entering in, we become an answer to the prayer of compassion. You may not become the founder of a major organization like Bob Pierce, but you and I don't have to be. We just have to be faithful to what Jesus has already asked and pray, "Lord Jesus, send more workers into your harvest field."

# Getting Away With Jesus

1. Think about a time when you were motivated to help someone in their distress. What was it that touched your heart and what type of action did you take to help?

_____

_____

_____

2. What are some of the things that cause your heart to break? How can you take action to help in both a temporal and eternal way?

_____

_____

_____

3. Who were the people who shared the gospel with you? Take some time to thank the Lord for sending them to you, and consider writing them a note, or giving them a call to encourage them.

_____

_____

_____

# 2
# Enlarging Our Hearts

I've reached an age where my personal physician is giving me new medical advice. In addition to concluding my yearly exam with words such as, "I'd like to see you do something about your weight," and "are you exercising?" he's now saying, "I'd like you to take a baby aspirin every day." The former words are the result of too many second helpings. The latter is the result of age. Since I'm getting older, my doctor realizes that my physical heart requires some precautionary maintenance. His goal is to keep me "heart-healthy". My doctor wants to keep my blood flowing and my heart pumping the way it was designed to work. Hence the push for less eating, more exercise, and those nasty little orange pills that create flashbacks of childhood illnesses. And, just like certain measures are prescribed to keep our physical hearts functioning the way they were designed, similar principles apply to our spiritual hearts. Including a healthy, growing Christ-like compassion for those harassed and helpless like sheep without their Shepherd.

One reason to desire a healthy, growing spiritual heart is the ongoing transformation that God is making in our lives as a new creation in Christ. A verse from Romans states, "For those God foreknew He also predestined to be conformed to the likeness of His Son...." (Rom. 8:29, NIV) Part of being conformed (or transformed) into the likeness of Christ is to have His compassion for the lost. The type of compassion that results in action. This leads to a second reason for keeping our spiritual hearts healthy.

Since the prayer request of Christ emerged from His heart of compassion, our hearts will need Christ-like compassion if we're to be an ongoing answer to the Lord's request. When writing on this topic the late South-African minister and author Andrew Murray penned the following:

> Solemn thought! O why is it that we do not obey the injunction of the Master more heartily, and cry more earnestly for labourers? There are two reasons. The first one is: We miss the compassion of Jesus, which gave rise to this request for prayer."[1] (*The second we will look at in Chapter Four.*)

To help avoid missing the compassion of Jesus, we'll devote this chapter to suggesting some ideas for seeking the Lord to enlarge our heart of compassion toward the lost – the seeds of which we've already been given.

## GOOD NEWS OF A GOD HEART

One afternoon, while watching a missions message given by pastor and author David Platt,[2] I noticed how he appeared deeply burdened with the thought of people dying who've never heard the name of Christ. When I saw his apparent brokenness I wondered, "Why don't I have a similar burden?" As I reflected on that moment, a couple of thoughts took shape.

First, I was able to remember certain times in my life where I did experience a greater sense of concern and compassion toward those without Christ. Second, I began realizing how God was using this video to inspire me to increase my compassion toward the lost. He wasn't using the message I watched as an instrument of condemnation, but an instrument of invitation. An invitation to open my heart to the Holy Spirit, asking Him and allowing Him to enlarge my heart and increase the desires He'd already given me. The same can be true for you.

If you're a believer who's not sensing much Christ-like compassion toward unbelievers, but would like to, this desire is your invitation. It's also indicative that God is at work in your heart. Scripture says, "For it is God who is working in you, (enabling you) both to will and to act for His good purpose." (Phil. 2:13, HCSB) Therefore, if you desire your compassion toward unbelievers to increase, that desire has been placed there by Christ. It's a response to the way God is working in your life, which is good news. And there's more! There's additional good news in that verse from Philippians. It's a promise that's found in the word "both." God is not only working to gives us certain desires such as Christ-like compassion, He's also working in our lives to enable us to act on these desires and bring them to fruition. God doesn't give us divine desires in order to frustrate us. He gives us these desires because He's also going to enable us to work out what He's begun.

The following verses, one from the Old Testament and one from the New, reveal more good news about our new "God-heart." A heart already containing the seeds of Christ-like compassion, that are waiting to blossom in each of the Lord's followers.

> I will give you a new heart and put a new spirit within you; I will remove your heart of stone and give you a heart of flesh. I will place My Spirit within you and cause you to follow My statutes and carefully observe My ordinances.
>
> (Ezek. 36:26-27, HCSB)

> ... Because God's love has been poured out in our hearts through the Holy Spirit who was given to us.
>
> (Rom. 5:5, HCSB)

The day you and I trusted Christ to take away our sins and give us eternal life, He also gave us a new heart. A God-heart filled with His love and a place where the Holy Spirit resides. This doesn't mean we've become God, or that we ever will. What it does mean is that the Lord has given our hearts a makeover, making it alive in Christ with a new nature just like His. A heart created in His image, with the potential to desire what He does. The verse from Romans states that God has "poured" His love into our hearts. This is an unlimited love that surpasses knowledge. (Eph. 3:19) And this love is not only the love He has *for you*. It's also the love He has *for others*. A love that's designed to grow and touch lives, as indicated by a prayer the Apostle Paul prayed for the church in Thessalonica: "And may the Lord cause you to increase and overflow with love for one another and for everyone, just as we also do for you." (1 Thess. 3:12, HCSB)

So whether our Christ-like compassion is waiting to emerge, whether it's been there for a while, or whether you've sensed it from time to time and want it to increase, we're all in need of the Holy Spirit to continue working in our hearts. Keeping us "heart-healthy" so that our hearts will increase and overflow with compassion. Just as Christ intended.

## CLEANSING OUR HEARTS

When my doctor recommends that I lose a few pounds, he's advising me to remove something harmful from my life. Something that can potentially cause a hardening of my physical heart and prevent it from beating the way it's designed. The same is true with our spiritual hearts. And one of the things that can harden our spiritual hearts isn't really a secret. It's sin, plain and simple.

When there's sin in our lives that we aren't willing to confess and renounce, our spiritual hearts will harden and turn away from the things of God. Now more than ever, it seems that we need to be on our guard as the world around us sprints further away from Biblical principles, seeking to influence us with an interest for things that aren't from our Father. (1 John 2:15-17) Complicating this, and adding confusion to the challenges and temptations aimed at our sinful desires, is that many who claim to follow Christ embrace some of the very same sins that the world does. In doing so, many utilize fine-sounding arguments that can deceive us and take us away from a sincere and pure devotion to Christ. (See Col. 2:8 and 2 Cor. 11:3-4). If we accept, endorse, and/or compromise with the world's lifestyle, we first and foremost grieve the Holy Spirit within us. We will also harden our spiritual hearts, making them dull and apathetic toward the lost and placing us in danger of missing Christ's compassion.

The good news in regard to sin is not the sin, but the Lord's mercy as found in the following promise. "If we confess our sins, He is faithful and righteous to forgive us our sins and to cleanse us from all unrighteousness." (1 John 1:9, HCSB) That verse is not an endorsement to live in a habitual pattern of sin-confess-sin-confess, but a truth that no matter what we've done, the blood of Christ gives us the ongoing invitation to turn from our fallen ways and be forgiven. And by keeping what many call "short accounts" with God, keeping our hearts cleansed through regular examination (Psalm 139:23-24) and confession, our spiritual arteries are now prepared for more proactive measures. Spiritual exercises that can help increase our love and compassion toward others.

## OUR FIRST CALL

Two men who heard Jesus' prayer request were Peter and his brother Andrew. They were two of the twelve apostles, and also two of the first answers to Christ's request. (See Matt. 10:1) When Jesus called them to be part of His initial disciples, one of the things He said was, "Follow Me, and I will make you fishers of men." (Matt. 4:19) Their call reveals the sequence for being an answer. It began with the call to follow Jesus. To know Him, walk with Him, learn from Him, to be in a growing, vibrant relationship with Christ Himself. It's the first thing you and I are called to as well. Jesus summarized the essence of eternal life as a relationship with God. "And this is eternal life, that they know You, the only true God, and Jesus Christ whom You have sent." (John 17:3) From this relationship, their ministry (and ours) to others would emerge. And it's from a growing relationship with Christ, that our hearts will enlarge and become more like His. Without this growing relationship, our hearts are certain to harden.

One year, while I was teaching on evangelism in the nation of Uganda, a man came up to me in between sessions with a big smile on his face and said the following.

"I'm an evangelist too, and I love to share the gospel, but it used to be such a burden." I looked at him and asked, "What made the difference? What caused it (sharing the gospel) to go from a burden to a joy?"

Without hesitating, and still smiling he answered, "Oh, I started spending more time with God than I did with people!" His words made such an impact on me, that I shared them with the group in our next session. I've also shared them everywhere I've taught on evangelism. What this man said not only challenged me in regard to my own walk with Christ, they reminded me that a growing relationship with Christ gives us a greater desire and love for people without Him. By spending time with the Lord we get in touch with Jesus' heart and when we get in touch with His heart, our hearts will change. Our compassion toward the lost will increase, and being an answer by praying will become more and more a way of life.

## A NEW COMMAND

It's easy to overlook an important aspect of a healthy spiritual heart. As we seek a growing Christ-like compassion for those who are lost, it's easy to forget what is of equal … make that of greater importance: a grow-

ing love for those who already belong to Christ. We're instructed to "....
do good to everyone, and especially to those who are of the household of
faith." (Gal. 6:10). If we also revisit an earlier verse in this chapter, the one
where the Apostle Paul shared a prayer that he had for the church in Thessalonica, we'll notice that he prayed for the church to have an increasing
and overflowing love. One that began with love for one another, and then
extends to an increasing love for everyone. This reflects back to what Jesus
mentioned in a pre-cross command: "I give you a new commandment:
love one another. Just as I have loved you, you must also love one another.
By this all people will know that you are My disciples, if you have love for
one another." (John 13:34-35, HCSB)

How often I tend to forget that our very first evangelistic principle
appears to originate from those very words. Jesus has promised that if
we love one another as He loved us, the world will know that we're His
followers. Perhaps they won't admit it, but they'll know it. And many will
be attracted by this when they see it. The theme of loving one another permeates the New Testament. It's a part of the Great Commandment (Mark
12:28-31), and is highlighted by the Apostle John in one of his later letters.
"Now this is His command: that we believe in the name of His Son Jesus
Christ, and love one another as He commanded us." (1 John 3:23, HCSB).
And, since this is a command from Christ, and a very important part of the
way we're portrayed to the world, then I believe we can say it will have an
effect on whether our compassion to the lost grows or stagnates as well.
As our love grows for those within the body of Christ – not just for those
within our own local church, but also toward those in other churches – it's
only natural that this is an important and necessary step if our hearts are
going to grow in Christ-like compassion toward the lost.

## JUST ASK

Take a moment and fill in the blank.

"You are what you _____."

Some might respond, "You are what you are." Others are familiar with
the saying, "You are what you eat." I'd like to fill in that blank by saying,
"You are what you pray." Oswald Chambers wrote, "Modern disciples....
need to concentrate more on how prayer changes us and less on how it
changes things."[3] Therefore our spiritual hearts can remain healthy, and
also enlarge, by simply praying. By asking the Holy Spirit to change us,
and to increase the level of our compassion toward those without Christ.

The Bible says, "...You do not have, because you do not ask." (James 4:2) It also says, "And I tell you, ask, and it will be given to you; seek, and you will find; knock, and it will be opened to you." (Luke. 11:9) If we pray regularly, "Lord, I'm asking You to increase my heart of compassion toward the lost," we can expect Him to answer. When Bob Pierce asked the Lord for his heart to be broken with the things that broke the heart of God, it appears that God answered. Therefore, is there any reason He wouldn't answer you and me? Even if we already have a burden for the lost, continuing to ask the Lord for his heart is beneficial, as there's always room for growth. Plus, it keeps us humbly dependent upon His Spirit; since apart from Him we can do nothing.

This prayer can be an intimidating one. Something we may be hesitant to pray initially. That's likely the result of a couple of misconceptions regarding Christ-like compassion. One misconception might be the fear that if you ask for increased compassion, then you're going to spend all of your time weeping and emotionally distraught over other people's souls. Yet even those whom God may deeply burden in an emotional way (and one man I personally know comes to mind) will still laugh, enjoy, their families, even watch a movie, and root for their favorite sports team. If we do, however, shed tears over those without Christ, may it be welcomed as a good thing if and when God brings it about in our lives, even if only momentarily. And though emotional responses can and will vary, more than likely what you and I can expect is that our concern for souls will increase, causing us to pray more and be more intentional in helping reach others with the gospel. All of this is good - the sign of a healthy, growing heart, and a part of being transformed into Christ's image.

Another reason this prayer can be frightening is for the opposite reason of what we've just addressed. What if we "don't" get emotional regarding lost souls?

Experiencing emotion, even shedding tears from time to time, are good things, to be welcomed as a gift from God. But this prayer and the others in this chapter are a matter of faith, obedience, and our will, and not dependent on our feelings. Because God has created us to experience emotions, it's easy to forget that the foundation for a transformed life begins with our minds, not with our feelings. "Be transformed by the renewal of your mind," writes Paul in the book of Romans. (Rom. 12:2) Therefore, the transformative process for increased compassion isn't centered on the way we're feeling, but on the way we're thinking. And one way to engage our minds in the area of compassion is to pray about the specific things we're talking about, even when we don't feel like it or sense anything happening.

When we pray based solely on the way we feel, we can be deceived into thinking the answers to our prayers are based more upon us than they are upon God. Feelings are great, but they come and go. The Bible tells us, "for we walk by faith, not by sight." (2 Cor. 5:7) When we pray based on the way we feel, it's more like sight-walking. When we pray based on the will and word of God it's faith-walking. And when we pray according to the will and Word of God, we're responding with what we know and have learned (our minds), becoming obedient by an act of our will. This brings us into faith-walking, which pleases God. (Heb. 11:6) I love sensing the presence of God, even an emotional connection with Him when I pray. I'm learning, however, that I must remain faithful in prayer regardless of the way I'm feeling – that I must pray and not give up, just like Jesus taught. (Luke 18:1) I must pray believing that if I seek a heart like Jesus, He'll not only give it, He'll enlarge it.

Depending on your personality type, you may not shed tears or get overly emotional, but your interest in the souls of men and women will increase. You'll begin thinking more about the eternal state of people. Even if feelings are absent, we can trust the Lord to be working in ways that will indeed enlarge our hearts. "We don't have because we don't ask." "We will have, if we do ask."

## PRAYING FOR PEOPLE BY NAME

Another way for the Holy Spirit to massage our hearts is by praying for people by name. The Apostle Paul wrote,

> Brothers, my heart's desire and prayer to God for them
> (the nation of Israel) is that they may be saved. (Rom. 10:1)

Paul prayed for people to come to Jesus. He desired their salvation. Do we? Do we each have a list of people we pray for on a regular basis to come to a saving faith in Jesus Christ? If you do, then according to the following passage, your prayers are connected to the desires of God.

> First of all, then, I urge that supplications, prayers, inter-
> cessions, and thanksgivings be made for all people, for kings
> and all who are in high positions, that we may lead a peaceful
> and quiet life, Godly and dignified in every way. This is good,

and it is pleasing in the sight of God our Savior, who desires all people to be saved and to come to the knowledge of the truth.

(1 Tim. 2:1-4)

In those verses, the first type of prayer listed is a supplication. Asking the Lord to increase our Christ-like compassion would be a supplication.

Then there's intercession, or prayers for others and the passage above directs us to pray "for all people," with a major emphasis being their salvation. This is indicated by the words, "God our Savior, who desires all people to be saved and to come to the knowledge of the truth." (v.3-4) If you're like me, it is a lot easier to pray for family and friends to be saved. It's harder to pray for those who aren't that close to us. But, by broadening the number of people we ask the Father to draw to Christ (John 6:44) we're aligning our prayers with the desire of God's heart: a desire for "all people." In doing so, we're exercising our spiritual hearts, allowing the Holy Spirit to enlarge them, giving us a greater burden and desire for people without Christ.

## THE PRAYER OF COMPASSION

Praying for Christ to give us His heart, and praying for people to be saved, are two ways that the Holy Spirit can massage our hearts and give it a compassion workout. Praying the prayer of compassion and asking Christ to send workers into the harvest can impact our hearts as well. It was compassion that prompted the Lord to ask us to ask Him to send more workers into this ever-growing, harvest field. Since His prayer appeal was rooted in His Heart, then praying this prayer can touch our hearts too. "It will lead us into the fellowship of that compassionate heart of His that led Him to call for our prayers."[4]

Think about the things you regularly pray about. More than likely it is something or someone who's very important to you. Our prayers are naturally motivated by what we're most passionate about, interested in, and concerned about. Sending workers into the harvest is something Jesus is passionate about, interested in, and concerned about. The Bible says, "Delight yourself in the LORD, and He will give you the desires of your heart." (Psalm 37:4) As we pray for the things the Lord is concerned about, that's one way to delight ourselves in Him. We're promised that in doing so, He will give us the desire of our hearts. Therefore, if the desire of our heart is to grow in Christ-like compassion, by praying for Christ to send more workers, we can expect Him to answer by sending these workers, and by deepening our burden for people as well.

The prayers we've looked at are three spiritual exercises that can enlarge our spiritual hearts in the same way physical exercise enlarges our natural hearts. This may not happen overnight but as Paul writes, "Let us not become weary in doing good, for at the proper time we will reap a harvest if we do not give up." (Gal. 6:9, NIV) I don't know why God seems to bring a harvest when He does. But His design for bringing one that you and I experience is based on our remaining faithful even when the answers we seek arrive slowly. We may not know how God is working; we may not sense things right away, and we may not see all those we pray for come to Christ for many years. But when we pray according to His will, He hears us and, in His perfect time He'll answer.


## REPLACEMENT PRAYERS

Jesus said to "watch and pray." (Mark 14:38) Paul wrote, "Devote yourselves to prayer, being watchful and thankful." (Col. 4:2, NIV) To watch means to stay awake and alert. As we seek for Christ to enlarge our hearts, it will be beneficial for us to watch. To stay alert regarding some of the things that might hinder us from praying some of the prayers we've looked at already. It might be the way we feel. Perhaps it's forgetfulness. I certainly struggle with both. However, there's another, more subtle obstacle for us to be watching for. Something that can easily go unnoticed, yet hinders the Holy Spirit's work in our hearts, limiting our compassion. These watching prayers we're going to call "replacement prayers" and they involve the battles being waged in our minds. The battle to "take every thought captive to obey Christ." (2 Cor. 10:5)

The following verse is small but says a lot. "For as he thinks in his heart so is he." (Prov. 23:7, NKJV) How do you think in your heart, unless the mind and heart are closely related? To look at how this might work in relation to a growing Christ-like compassion, try giving yourself a little test. What kind of thoughts do you have toward people you see and interact with on a daily basis? Are they Christ-like or are they negative? What's the first thought that goes through your mind when you see someone walking along the street that looks a little different than you? Maybe they're a little disheveled, even a little dangerous. Is your first thought a negative one? How often do certain unflattering adjectives pop into your mind?

Or how about that certain neighbor, the one that makes you wish you had enough money to buy their home just so they would move. Or how about that favorite co-worker? The one that makes you want to quit your job, even in a down economy, just to get away from them. What are your thoughts toward these people? Negative, judgmental thoughts are actually thoughts based on our old nature, "the flesh." They're not the mind of Christ. The mind of Christ is thinking with compassion, seeing people as sheep without a Shepherd, whose "fingernails on the chalkboard" personality is a reflection of the helpless, hopeless hole they have in their hearts. If we allow the "fleshly" negative thoughts to take root, then the way we're thinking will make its way directly to our hearts and restrict the heart of compassion and brokenness Jesus placed within us.

Whenever you and I cross paths with a person who causes a "red alert" in our minds, instead of a negative thought, replace it with prayer. Something like, "Lord, I thank You that You love that person," or, "Father, draw that person to Your Son Jesus." It doesn't have to be complicated; a simple "prayer of compassion" toward someone can be far more powerful and beneficial than anything negative. The Bible teaches, "Finally brothers, whatever is true, whatever is honorable, whatever is just, whatever is pure, whatever is lovely, whatever is commendable, if there is any excellence, if there is anything worthy of praise, think about these things." (Phil. 4:8). When we combine that with the promise "love never fails", (1 Cor. 13:8, NIV) then replacing harsh thoughts with loving ones can help enlarge our hearts. Our compassion will grow and become more and more like the compassion Jesus had the day He looked upon the masses with a broken-heart.

## BEING A SEE-THROUGHER

Before moving on to one more exercise, I'd like to share the following excerpt. When I read it, it gave me a much clearer picture in regard to replacement praying, and a perspective to help transform our minds through the way we view other people. It comes from the book, *Chain Reactions, a Call to Compassionate Revolution*, by Darrell Scott* who shares the following comments made to him by an author named Norman Grubb.

> He (Grubb) stayed in my home numerous times when I was in my twenties and early thirties. I'll never forget a simple lesson he taught me as we were having a discussion one day. He said, "Darrell, we live in a world of illusions. If you really want to be

*Darrell Scott is the father of Rachel Scott, one of the students killed at Columbine High School in a tragic school shooting in 1998.*

43

fulfilled in life, you must learn to see through the illusions to the reality. If you will learn to be a 'see-througher' instead of a look 'atter', life will have far more meaning." That simple statement from Norman Grubb was to change my life forever.

Most of the time, people look at circumstances instead of seeing through them. We focus on the superficial surface instead of seeing the deeper reality. We judge others so easily by viewing their clothes, facial expressions, body language, and so forth, instead of taking a caring look at their hearts. Mercy triumphs over judgment when we learn to be a "see-througher."[5]

Jesus was a "see-througher." The Bible says, "For the LORD sees not as man sees: man looks on the outward appearance, but the LORD looks on the heart." (1 Samuel 16:7) When Jesus looked at people, He saw more than the outside; He saw the inside. This doesn't mean He condones sin, or will overlook it, but when Jesus sees people and is filled with compassion, He looks behind the clothes, facial expressions, successes or failures. He sees beyond gender, race, ethnicity, or economic status. Instead He's able to see the soul. He knows why He created them. He knows what they can be if they'll turn to Him. He was the ultimate "see-througher." And as you and I learn to see through, and pray replacement prayers, we allow the Holy Spirit to clean out our spiritual arteries and keep our spiritual hearts healthy.

## THE ANSWER BEGINS

As we make these prayers a regular part of our life, you and I have taken the first step in being an answer through prayer. But prayer alone won't fully develop a Christ-like heart. For that to happen we'll have to combine praying with going. By being one of the workers we're praying for Christ to send. Although Section Two is devoted to going, it's important for us to look at it in some of these early chapters … like this one.

In the Bible, prayer and action go hand and hand. On more than one occasion we read how the Lord told His servants to stop praying and take action. When the Israelites were locked in a vice grip with the Red Sea on one side and the Egyptian Army on the other, God spoke to the praying Moses, telling him to take action. "Why are you crying out to Me? Tell the Israelites to break camp. As for you, lift up your staff, stretch out your hand over the sea, and divide it so that the Israelites can go through the sea on dry ground." (Exod. 14:15-16, HCSB)

Another time, Joshua was seeking God for an answer regarding the defeat of the armies of Israel. The Lord eventually told Joshua to take action. (Josh. 7:10-13) Those two are certainly noteworthy and teach us a lot, yet there's one Biblical account where prayer and action really stand out: the cross of Christ. The book of Isaiah gives the following prophecy about Jesus, "For He bore the sin of many, and made intercession for the transgressors." (Isa 53:12, NIV) We read of the fulfillment of this prophecy when Jesus prayed from the cross, "Father, forgive them, for they do not know what they are doing." (Luke 23:34, NIV). On the cross, while Jesus was dying a brutal death, He also prayed. His action on the cross is what made the answer to His prayer a reality. Prayer precedes action, as well it should, but prayer and action go together, just as they did in the examples we've just cited. And just as prayer and action go together in many places in the Bible, they also go together as part of God's design for making us more like Jesus. For enlarging the God-heart that He's placed within us.

I remember taking an evangelism class offered by my church fifteen years ago. After the opening class, we were challenged to go out and put our learning into practice, which I did. With one of the people I spoke to, the phrase from Matthew, "sheep without a Shepherd" became very real.

I was teaching school at the time and approached a colleague to share the Gospel, using the methods we were taught in the class. As we were going through the Scriptures and I was listening to his responses, it became obvious that he knew very little about Jesus. He shared with me that one of his limited recollections of Christianity was a man standing on his college campus shouting at the girls and telling them they were going to hell for wearing makeup. My heart broke as I learned that his only knowledge of Christ was in relation to a "fashion-policeman" masquerading as a preacher. As I listened to him further the phrase, "sheep without a Shepherd" came rushing into my mind. The Lord was touching my heart and it wasn't the result of praying alone. It was the result of going into the harvest field. The result of putting "feet" on my prayers.

This is where Christ truly touches our hearts. This is where we experience Him on a deeper level. This is where those compassionate feelings we've been wondering about begin to surface. This is where our hearts grow larger and larger in Christ-like compassion. The Holy Spirit seems to massage our hearts the most through the experience of ministering to people. There's no doubt that praying is needed, but without the "going" we'll restrict the compassion that Christ wants to bring into our lives. Pastor and author Francis Chan shares the following:

> I'm excited about evangelism again. When I was in high school, I used to cry for my friends when I would think about spending eternity apart from them. When I was working in a restaurant, I used to cry over the other waiters and waitresses and think, "God, you gotta save these people!" When I worked in the church, I didn't weep a whole lot for the lost – it was just kind of sporadic. Now that I'm spending so much more time building relationships with unbelievers and loving on them, there are a lot more tears. There is a lot more sadness, a lot more urgency, and it's painful and can be depressing, and yet there's this peace about finally going out and fishing for men. It feels good to care so much and even hurt so much at times. I would encourage leaders not to get too caught up in methodology because once your heart breaks enough for people, you'll find a way to get the message to them.[6]

By spending time building relationships and loving on them the tears returned. And though Chan talks about sadness, urgency and being depressed, he talks about having a peace in fishing for men. In going himself. It's the result of a Christ-like heart. A heart familiar with sorrow, but a heart familiar with peace in seeking those who are lost. It was the result of "going" to the lost and the result was an enlarged heart.

## BIBLE OR REFRIGERATOR

Before moving on, let's do a quick review by making a list of the prayers we've stated in this chapter.

1) Asking Christ to increase our compassion for other believers and for the lost.

2) Praying for people by name to come to a saving faith in Jesus Christ.

3) Asking Christ to send more workers into His harvest field.

4) Praying Replacement Prayers.

In the Next Steps section in the back of the book, there's a sample copy of many of the things we place on the prayer cards that are used in our ministry. Cards that can help us remember to pray these prayers on a regular basis. Other things are included that relate to the "going" part of being an answer, and can be utilized in a way that can touch our hearts, as we also prepare to touch lives. But whether it's a card, or a photocopy of the page at the end of this chapter, or a note that you write out by hand, I'd like to encourage you to keep something where you can see it because, if you're like me, I often forget. Someone once suggested taking the prayer card and putting it in your Bible or on your refrigerator, whichever one you open more. Whatever works best for you, these suggestions are simply designed to help us in remembering to pray, and by prayer allow the Holy Spirit to increase our hearts toward those without Christ. I believe if you and I will pray like this on a regular basis, our spiritual hearts will stay healthy and also enlarge.

A Christ-like heart already resides in each of His followers. And as this heart grows, it will enable us to faithfully endure as an answer to the prayer request of Christ. In doing so, we'll not only grow in our relation ship with Him, but we'll also begin to make a worldwide impact for the kingdom of God. An impact that results as Jesus sends more and more workers into His harvest.

# Getting Away With Jesus

1. Is praying for Christ to increase your compassion a little intimidating? Why or why not?

_____

_____

_____

2. How does 1 John 3:16-18 challenge the way we're to love one another?

_____

_____

_____

3. Are you a see-througher? Be conscious of the opportunity to pray replacement prayers in the coming week.

_____

_____

_____

*For some practical steps as well as a sample resource for praying through what's been mentioned in this chapter, see the Next Steps section at the end of the book.*

# 3
# If You Pray, They Will Go

I have a good friend who's a missionary to unreached people groups. One weekend after praying over a map of the nation where he lives, he and his family sensed the Lord directing them to a certain area in order to pray. They prayed for the kingdom and glory of the Lord to come to that village, and for churches to be planted there. A couple of months later my friend met an indigenous man who had moved his family to that area to do a similar work and they have been co-laborers ever since.

Later while home on furlough my friend received the news that this same man had begun to visit a remote district with some other believers and were engaging the youth in that area. It was the same district my friend and his family had visited and prayed for a couple of years earlier. God had heard the prayers of my missionary friend and family and had sent another worker into these harvest fields

The prayers of my missionary friend sets the stage for the theme for this chapter. A theme of expectation. A Godly-Confidence that if we ask Christ to send workers into the harvest field, we can expect Him to do so. And by praying we can help make a worldwide impact for the glory of God. In fact, our prayers can be offered with such expectation we can say with faith, "If you pray, they will go."

## FIELDS OF PROMISE

Depending on your age and your interest in movies, the phrase "If you pray, they will go" might sound familiar. It's adapted from a Hollywood movie released in 1989 by Universal Studios titled "Field of Dreams." The movie starred Kevin Costner, and had the memorable line "If you build it, he will come." These instructions were given to Costner, who played the role of a fictitious Iowa farmer. In the film, Costner's character was being called upon to build a baseball diamond in his cornfield. If Costner built the baseball diamond, then Shoeless Joe Jackson (who was suspended from major league baseball in 1921) would magically appear. Costner built the field and eventually, not only Jackson appears, but also many other former major leaguers who begin playing baseball on this mid-western farm. Costner built the field and the game was on. He acted upon the instructions he heard and the promise became a reality.

Since the above-mentioned movie was fiction, if you plan on building a baseball field in your backyard, you may want to invite a few "living" players or it's going to be a pretty boring game. I would, however, like to use the principle behind the phrase "if you build it, he will come" and apply it to the prayer request of Christ. Here's why. If you and I act upon our Lord's instructions and pray for Him to send workers into His harvest, we too can expect an answer. So much so, that our slogan for being an answer through prayer can be stated like this: "If you pray, they (the workers) will go."

## BEING AN ANSWER LEADS TO ANSWERS

When Jesus gave His request for workers, He began His appeal with the following words, "Therefore, pray earnestly, the Lord of the harvest." (Matt. 9:38) The strength of that statement, and the reason we can expect our prayers will be heard and answered, rests in the truth that Jesus is Lord. He is the Master, the One with complete authority in the harvest field. Since Jesus is the One with all authority, He has the right to determine the divine design for reaching the world. And His perfect plan and design begins with prayer. Prayer is the catalyst that moves Christ to move people who move into the harvest to seek the lost, and care for them when they're found. Therefore, you and I can pray expectantly. We can pray knowing that by being an answer through prayer, it leads to many answers who will go. The following verses provide additional encouragement for praying this "sending" prayer with expectancy.

This is the confidence we have in approaching God: that if we ask anything according to His will, He hears us. And if we know that He hears us-- whatever we ask-- we know that we have what we asked of Him. (1 John 5:14-15, NIV)

John wrote that if we ask "anything" according to God's will, then God hears us and gives us what we've asked Him for. When we pray for Christ to send workers, this is a prayer that sits squarely in the center of God's will. If it didn't, Christ wouldn't have given the command. When Jesus walked the earth He said, "For I have come down from heaven not to do My own will but to do the will of Him who sent Me." (John 6:38, NIV) Since Jesus was perfect and never sinned, this means that everything He ever did, every thought He ever had, every word He ever spoke, even all of His innermost motives, rested squarely in His Father's will – including this command to pray. This is why we can state with confidence, "If you pray, they will go."

## "THEY WILL GO AND THEY ARE NEEDED"

Prior to Jesus giving His request, Matthew wrote, "… when He saw the crowds …" Though the population of the Galilean region during the time of Christ is uncertain, it's likely this was a densely populated area. Large enough for Jesus to give His appeal by pointing out that "the harvest is plentiful."

Fast forward from that moment in Matthew to the 21st century and the crowds are increasing. Over seven billion people are alive today on planet earth, and the number is growing. Of these seven billion, close to three billion (over 40 percent) are classified as "unreached" with the gospel.* The word "unreached" can be defined in different ways, but for the most part the term represents people living in places with minimal or no access to Christ's good news. Whenever I travel overseas, it seems like the words of Jesus, "the harvest is plentiful, but the workers are few" is an understatement. People, opportunities, and needs are everywhere. And it's not just the result of sheer numbers; specific needs are prevalent too.

I just visited a friend in another nation. He directs a soccer ministry that began by reaching out to kids on the street. Another friend has a growing elementary school, hoping to provide an education to poorer children. Cross the border of that country into a neighboring nation and

*These are approximations based on statistics viewed at www.JoshuaProject.net

work is just now beginning on the first-ever Bible translation in the local dialect. And as I write, I'm reminded of the ministry of Forward Edge International and a specific work they have in Nicaragua, called the "Villa Esperanza" (Village of Hope). Through this ministry, many young girls have found a refuge from poverty, despair, and even child prostitution. I had the privilege of spending the night at the "Villa" one year and meeting some of the girls and staff; it's an amazing work of God. (For more information visit forwardedge.org)

What's described above are just a few of the needs I've witnessed first-hand, that cover just a few places, in a few countries. Suffice it to say that in our present day, the request of Christ speaks louder than ever, as more and more workers are needed for a job that's large and growing.

The size of the task isn't just an international issue; it's a local issue as well. I remember my years as a teacher in Ohio's public schools. One day as I supervised close to 700 students in our cafeteria during lunch time, I remember having a sense of compassion toward these teens. The following verse came to mind: "...And how can they hear without someone preaching to them?" (Rom. 10:14, NIV) Sitting right there before me, at table after table in a maroon-carpeted lunch room, was a harvest field in need of workers. So whether we're at home or in another nation – everywhere we go, the harvest task is a large one and it's growing. And since the design and will of the Lord is for prayer to precede sending, then more than ever Christ-followers are needed to be an answer through prayer.

Before becoming discouraged by the size of the task, there is good news in the words, "the harvest is plentiful." These words not only represent the size of the task, but the promise within the task. The promise is that when Christ sends workers, He'll send them to places where He's already working, preparing to touch hearts and change lives.


## LARGE FIELD, LARGE PROMISE

The word "harvest," as related to the present age before Christ returns, is defined in a couple of ways. One, "of the gathering of men into the kingdom of God," and another, "a multitude of men to be taught how to obtain salvation."[1] When we pray, the Lord sends workers and eventually men and women are taught the way of salvation and this gathering occurs. In the gospel of John we read an account that illustrates the principle of harvest readiness in the town of Sychar, located in Samaria.

One day as Jesus left Judea for Galilee, He intentionally routed His followers through Sychar. Since Samaritans didn't get along well with the Jewish people, and the Lord's disciples were Jewish, I'm sure expectations were low on this part of the journey. To their surprise, what began with Jesus reaching out to a promiscuous woman avoided by many in town, ended up igniting a city-wide harvest. In between the Lord's encounter with this woman and the eventual two-day outreach Jesus had with the townsfolk, the Lord took the time to teach some valuable harvest principles – principles that applied then, and still apply today. Principles that are relevant where we live, as well as in other nations. Jesus said, "Do you not say, 'Four months more and then the harvest?' I tell you, open your eyes and look at the fields! They are ripe for harvest." (John 4:35 NIV) In other words, the harvest for souls isn't just a future event. The fields are ready NOW! Jesus gave proof of this shortly thereafter when the town of Sychar became the home of many new believers.

One reason the fields were harvest-ready that day in Samaria, was due to what others had done previously. Immediately after telling the disciples that the fields were "ripe," Jesus said the following:

> Even now the reaper draws his wages, even now he harvests the crop for eternal life so that the sower and the reaper may be glad together. Thus the saying, 'One sows and another reaps' is true. I sent you to reap what you have not worked for. Others have done the hard work, and you have reaped the benefits of their labor. (John 4:36-38, NIV)

Those words magnify the need for you and me to be an answer, since they reveal that the harvest normally occurs through a process. "Rome wasn't built in a day," and neither is the harvest. Some workers are sent to sow and may not know how the Lord used them until eternity. Certain missionary biographies inform us of people who labored long and hard before seeing a result, some even giving their lives as part of the "ground-breaking" part of the harvest. They were sent for a purpose because people were praying. Others are sent to reap, like the disciples that day in Sychar. Some will do a little of both, but whatever their Christ-ordained role, they were sent because someone prayed. Consistent prayer moved Christ to send workers to sow, and workers to reap, and many to do a little of both. So regardless of the will of God for those He sends, the promise still stands, "the harvest" is plentiful. The Holy Spirit is at work and whether the gathering takes place today, tomorrow or in ten years, those whom the Lord sends, are going to places where the Holy Spirit is working and carrying out a plan. The task is large, but it's also promising and "if you pray, they will go."

## THE PROMISE BECOMES A REALITY

As we drove to a village in Southern India, I was excited. Our host pastor had a small team working in the area and had informed me that many who lived there had little to no knowledge of Jesus. With three thousand people living in this village, I was blessed by the opportunity the Lord had given me.

The villagers were in bondage to idol worship and as we entered one of the villages, we drove past trees where some of these idols were hanging in small bags held by ropes. To be able to present to these villagers the grace and love of the Son of God was an answer to a prayer I had prayed many years earlier. I had asked the Lord to send me someday to a place where people had never heard about Jesus. Some in that village would certainly be in this category.

We finally arrived at the location for our meeting and as I got out of the car, I was approached by a man who was speaking rapidly. I turned to our host pastor, who translated his words.

"He's telling you that his father died, his mother's near death, and that he's afraid to die."

"Would you ask him to have a seat," I told the pastor, pointing toward the chairs in a nearby field. "Tell him that I'm going to be talking about that tonight." The man listened as the pastor shared my words and decided to join our service.

Later that evening I gave a message on the supremacy of Christ from Colossians Chapter One. As the message ended and we invited people to turn from their sins and receive Christ, this man was one of the people wishing to do so. That was on a Friday night. Two days later on Sunday we returned with the host pastor and his team to hold the first-ever church service in that village. The man who had met me at the car two nights before and made a commitment to Christ, attended the Sunday service. He sat attentively toward the front of the group with a pink towel wrapped around his shoulders listening to the message. When the host pastor asked the people who had trusted Christ if they wanted to be baptized, this man was one of the people who stood up, indicating his desire to do so. According to what I've been told by some of those living in India, baptism is a major step, because it symbolizes a break from idolatry. It can lead to being ostracized by one's family, harassed and even persecuted by others, as it represents a break from past beliefs to follow Christ and Christ alone as Lord. This man was willing to take that step.

This man, like others we visited on this trip to India, revealed first-hand the reality of Jesus' words about the harvest. The Holy Spirit had certainly gone before us, preparing the way for people to hear the gospel and respond. The promise of the harvest being ready and ready now had come to life, and is coming to life even in places where the name of Jesus is relatively unknown. A process might be involved, but the Holy Spirit is at work, fulfilling a promise Jesus made to his disciples: "And I have other sheep that are not of this fold. I must bring them also, and they will listen to My voice. So there will be one flock, one Shepherd." (John 10:16)

## A SPECIFIC STRATEGY

The divine strategy laid out in Scripture is for prayer to precede sending, and sending results in the harvest. Since praying precedes sending, behind every worker that goes to the mission field is a prayer. And behind every person that speaks to a friend, I believe we'll find a prayer God used inspiring that person to go. Most likely it is the prayer of a family member. Think of your own journey to Christ; who spoke with you, or gave you a Bible or Christian literature of any type? Who invited you, or took you to church, where someone else, living out their sending was behind the podium speaking? Or who got your attention because "they seemed to have something you didn't"? The Apostle Paul once wrote, "What then is Apollos? What is Paul? Servants through whom you believed, as the Lord assigned to each. I planted, Apollos watered, but God gave the growth." (1 Cor. 3:5-6) Who were some of these planting, watering servants in your life? And who do you know that may have been praying for you, and as a result, the Lord sent someone to bring the good news into your life?

Just five years into my own walk with Christ, I shared the gospel with someone who made a profession of faith. The very next day this person told me that they had gone home that day and shared the news with their grandmother - a grandmother who just happened to be in prayer for her grandchild at the exact time that we had been talking about Jesus. The Bible says, "the prayer of a righteous person has great power as it is working." (James 5:16) And our prayers will work as the part of the Lord's design in sending someone to those who are close to us.

There's no question that the prayer request of Christ is important to world missions. It's also important where we live and work among the individuals in our community. And just as we pray for people by name to turn from their sin and trust Christ, we can also pray for workers to be sent to specific places in our communities. Praying in a general way is fine, but praying for specific people and places can be highly effective.

What do you have your greatest spiritual concern over? A school? An area of your city? A local university or its professors? How about friends and family living across the country? We can ask the Lord to raise up and send workers into specifically named places such as...

- Our cities and areas of the city.
- Our schools by name.
- Our government offices and officials.
- A specific region or area of a country.
- Our friends and family members.

I have a pastor and church prayer list. One of the things I pray is that God will raise up and send workers into the harvest with an open door for the gospel from these churches. Often I tag one of the above areas to my prayer. What kind of impact might be made if we begin to pray for Christ to raise up workers from our churches, even asking this for people we know by name? What kind of impact might be made in our communities if we ask for people to go into the specific places such as those listed above? And what kind of impact would be made on reaching the world, especially the unreached areas by praying for workers to go to countries, and people groups by name?

Is there a certain country you have a burden for? A great way to pray for that nation is to ask the Lord to send workers to help reach that nation. One year in Rwanda, a Rwandese woman shared with me that every time she prayed, the nation of Switzerland came to her mind. Perhaps she's to go there herself. Or perhaps she's to pray for Christ to reach Switzerland, and to do so by sending workers. Workers from among the Christians living in Switzerland, and workers from other nations too. Maybe she's to pray "and" also go herself. But even if this woman never leaves East Africa, through prayer she can make a kingdom impact on the continent of Europe. So can we.

## SENDING TOOLS

To help us extend our impact through specific prayer, there are a number of resources available. One resource which can help us make a worldwide impact is the book *Operation World*. This publication contains a thorough listing of every country in the world, with various statistics and prayer needs for each. Not only can this book help guide you in praying for specific countries, but also, as you read the facts and needs associated with each country, you'll gain a greater understanding of what Jesus meant when He said, "The harvest is plentiful." It will also grip your heart and inspire you to pray fervently as you gain little insights into each nation and their needs.

A second resource can be found through a ministry called the Joshua Project. If you go to the website JoshuaProject.net, you can access a lot of information regarding unreached people groups. They even have an app called "JP Unreached" that can be downloaded to a smartphone or tablet. I have one on each of my mobile devices and every day I can click on the app and receive information about a people group to pray for. It not only gives the name of the people, but their country and numerous other facts, such as whether there's a completed Bible in their language, and the availability of the "Jesus" film.* While typing these words I stopped to click on the group for today. It was a day to pray for the Namasudra – these are Hindu people who live in Bangladesh. Through resources like this, we are able to get in touch with countries as well as learn of people living in remote, isolated places.

Think how exciting it will it be to get to heaven and meet someone who was inspired to take the gospel somewhere in the world as a result of your prayers. I'm truly expecting that, and why not? Is there any reason God wouldn't use your prayers and mine in this way? The Bible says, "Now to Him who is able to do far more abundantly than all that we ask or think, according to the power at work within us, to Him be glory in the church and in Christ Jesus throughout all generations, forever and ever. Amen." (Eph. 3:20-21) If something will bring glory to God, and more workers in the harvest can certainly do that, then God can do far beyond what we're asking him to do in the harvest. Is there any reason He wouldn't do it with my prayers or with yours? The authority of Christ as Lord gives us reason to expect this.

1 John 5:14-15 also gives us this confident expectation, whether it's a prayer for another land, or a prayer for our neighborhoods: "This is the con-

---

* *A film based on the Gospel of Luke that's been viewed in every country and can be downloaded and viewed through the internet in multiple languages. For more information visit www.cru.org*

fidence we have in approaching God: that if we ask anything according to His will, He hears us. And if we know that He hears-- whatever we ask-- we know that we have what we asked of Him." (1 John 5:14-15, NIV) Imagine the effect on world evangelization and missions if every follower of Christ took this by faith and became an answer to the prayer request of Christ.

## IF YOU PRAY, THEY WILL PRAY

As we make our way toward the end of the chapter, we're going to take a little side road. Our destination is still the same, "if you pray, they will go," but there are a couple additional ingredients that will give this prayer principle a little "kick." By God's grace, I've been praying for the Lord to send workers. It's also been one of the heartbeats and themes of our ministry. But until working on this book, I had missed something very important that brings another dimension to our prayer for workers. While continuing to read from the writings of Andrew Murray, one of his prayers on the subject caught my attention.

> Lord, breathe Thine own Spirit on all Thy children, that they may learn to live for this one thing alone—the Kingdom and glory of their Lord—and become fully awake to what their prayer can accomplish. And let all our hearts be filled with the assurance that prayer, offered in loving faith in the living God, will bring certain and abundant answer. Amen.[2]

The line, "become fully awake to what their prayer can accomplish" caused an awakening in my own mind and heart. Not only can you and I pray for the Lord to send workers, but another prayer that's certainly deserving of a spot on our prayer list is that through the Spirit of God, more and more followers of Christ will begin to make the prayer of sending a priority in their lives.

## SEND ME

In the Old Testament, a man named Isaiah has a "no-holds barred" encounter with God. (Isa. 6:1-7) Afterwards, Isaiah shares what happened next. "And I heard the voice of the Lord saying, "Whom shall I send, and who will go for us?" Then I said, "Here am I! Send me." (Isa. 6:8) In Isaiah's life, the majesty of God led to the mercy of God, which led to a mission from God, and Isaiah volunteered to answer the Lord's question. Now, many years later, the eye of the Lord is still looking for people to send. And this sending is the normal outflow of what He's asked us to pray.

In the gospel of Matthew, right after Jesus issues His prayer request, he calls His twelve disciples and a few verses later we read, "These twelve Jesus sent out." (Matt. 10:5). In the gospel of Luke, the prayer request of Christ is listed again. Only now, instead of addressing the twelve apostles, Jesus is now addressing a group of seventy-two. Immediately after telling His followers to ask Him for workers, Jesus says the following: "Go your way; behold, I am sending you out as lambs in the midst of wolves." (Luke 10:3) As Lord of the harvest, Jesus begins by telling people to pray.

Then the very followers He told to pray, are the same ones He told to go. It's probably safe to say that these initial groups not only prayed for workers, but added the following words to their prayers. "Lord, send me too!" This adds a whole new dimension to our statement, "If you pray, they will go." Now, it can also be stated, "If you pray, you will go."

One Sunday after speaking from Luke Chapter 10, a person approached me who was very transparent. They told me how they'd known for years that the Lord wanted them to pray for the sending of workers, but they haven't done so. Why not? The fear that if they prayed that prayer, God would send them and they were hesitant about going. The more I spoke with this person, the more it appeared that their concern was that God would send them overseas. However, throughout our conversation I could sense this person was beginning to soften and also accept that possibility. God was slowly bringing them to a point of obedience. This is where the so-called "rubber meets the road," as the prayer request of Christ isn't designed just for us to pray; it's also designed for us to go – to become a complete answer.

Asking Christ to send workers into the harvest will not only impact others, it will also impact us. God may or may not send you overseas, but He may inspire you to be more active in your present centers of influence. He may not send you overseas long-term, but on a short-term mission's project that will touch lives and deepen your relationship with Christ. The Lord of the harvest, Jesus Christ, is the one who tells us to pray, and who also gives us the subsequent command to go. And Jesus is bigger than any of our fears. It doesn't mean we won't have fear; it only means that Jesus enables us to overcome them.

If all this puts a little "lump in your throat" that's a good thing ... for all of us. Those lumps are what keep you and me dependent on God, so that we depend on His strength and not our own. And those lumps serve to remind us that God always promises His divine enabling so that we can fulfill His divine commands. In the Book of Hebrews we read,

> Now may the God of peace who brought again from the dead our Lord Jesus, the great Shepherd of the sheep, by the blood of the eternal covenant, equip you with everything good that you may do His will, working in us that which is pleasing in His sight, through Jesus Christ, to whom be glory forever and ever. Amen. (Heb. 13:20-21)

Part of what He will be working in us, is whatever is necessary for you and I to be an answer – an answer by praying, and an answer by going. (More on this in Chapter Five.)

In 1989 Universal Studios released "Field of Dreams." Two thousand years earlier, in the region of Galilee, Jesus released a "field of promises" and did so through a prayer request. We become an answer to His prayer of compassion by praying, and as we do He'll inspire others to step on to this field of promise. And as we combine our praying by going, just like the early disciples, we too step on to this field and become a complete answer to the prayer request of Christ. These promises are based on the Lordship of Christ and His perfect design, His perfect will, and His perfect word, and because of Him, we can expectantly say: "If you pray, they will go." And by His grace, "If you pray, you will go."

Two great promises. Two great opportunities. As great as those opportunities are, they're probably not the greatest one in being an answer. Other opportunities exist related to faith, hope, and love, and are part of this call as well. These are things we'll look at in the next chapter, and lead us to the greatest reward of all.

# Getting Away With Jesus

1. Which country (countries) in the world do you find yourself thinking about a lot? Consider adopting those nations, praying for Christ to increase the number of workers there.

_____

_____

_____

2. Is there a part of your local community you have a burden for? How can you be an answer toward that part of your community?

_____

_____

_____

3. What steps need to be taken so that your church, Bible study, or small group can be an ongoing answer through prayer for your community and for the world? For help getting started, see the Next Steps section relating to this chapter.

_____

_____

_____

# 4
# Faith, Hope And Love

It was a casual Friday night in late October. I was involved in couch-potato multi-tasking with a book in one hand and the television remote nearby. That's when the phone rang. My wife Delores answered and l was surprised to hear that it was her son-in-law Jeff calling from San Diego, California. "Should I sit down?" Delores said jokingly as she rose from the sofa, walked out of the room and disappeared into my office.

Initially I didn't give the phone call much thought, but as time passed and Delores hadn't returned, I started thinking something might be wrong. I laid down my book, got out of the La-Z-Boy and walked to the office. When I entered the room I saw that Delores was still on the phone, with her head in her hand, crying. Immediately I went and put my arm around her and learned that her daughter Heather had been diagnosed with colon/rectal cancer. I picked up a second phone, listened a little, then announced my presence and asked if I could pray. It was the start of a journey no one anticipates, but drives you to your knees.

The following morning I sat at my computer and began recruiting people to pray. I sent e-mails to the U.S. and other countries sharing the news about Heather and asking as many as possible to pray on her behalf.

It wasn't long before responses from a variety of nations began arriving to tell me they would be praying. Some even shared their intentions to fast. There's no way to express sufficient gratitude for each and every person who prayed, whether it was a simple one-time prayer, to those who prayed fervently and frequently. Every person and every prayer was significant, meaningful and made a difference. There are, however, two people who prayed for Heather that are etched in my memory forever. Their example also provides a prayer principle that parallels the opportunity we have in praying sending prayers.

## ESTHER

A few months after that initial phone call, I traveled to East Africa. I was scheduled to minister in both Rwanda and Tanzania. Shortly after arriving in Rwanda, my good friend Pastor Augustine Butera told me that I needed to meet an older woman by the name of Esther. Esther lived in the region where a colleague and I were scheduled to conduct a city-wide evangelism festival. Though Esther and I had never met, she knew that I was coming to the city to minister. When she learned about Heather, Esther did something that not only astounded me, but many others who've heard the story. Esther not only prayed for Heather, she also fasted on her behalf for four days. That's not a misprint. Four days of prayer and fasting for someone she had only heard about.

My final day in this region, I had the privilege of visiting with Esther, her daughter, and a couple of friends. When Esther walked into the room you could sense a humble, quiet strength in her spirit just by the way she said hello. You could tell you were in the presence of an extremely Godly woman. After taking the time to get to know each other, I asked Esther if she would share her burden and experiences in praying for Heather. With her permission I recorded her comments on video so I could share them with others. It was an inspiration to those who've had the opportunity to watch it. Esther not only shared her burden, she also shared her tears, saying that when she cries, she knows that the Lord has heard her prayer.

## "STANDING IN THE GAP"

The following week, after meeting Esther, I traveled to Tanzania, and a city located near the base of Mount Kilimanjaro. One day, after a training seminar in personal evangelism, my interpreter wrote Heather's name on a piece of paper and asked me to hold it in front of the church. Two women then came up and laid their hands on my shoulders as the entire gathering began praying fervently for Heather. In both countries I was blessed by the way people were willing to pray – that they would pray intensely for what was important to me.

Four months later I returned to Tanzania for another city-wide evangelism festival. During the week, one of the host pastors informed me that a woman wanted to speak with me. On the final night of the festival, the pastor brought this woman to the place where I was sitting near the platform. I recognized her immediately. She was one of the ladies who put their hands on my shoulders in that church four months earlier and prayed for Heather. As she approached me she reached into her handbag and pulled out a piece of paper. It was the same paper that I held four months before as people prayed for Heather after our training session. This woman had kept the paper and had written on it Scripture references (Psalm 51 and Mark 11:23). She told me how she had been praying every day for Heather – that she was "standing in the gap" on Heather's behalf. Once again I was amazed at the way people, one a stranger, the other a brief acquaintance, had responded with such care and persistence, to my prayer requests.

I'm certain that the prayers of these women (and the many others who prayed) made a difference. Their diligent intercession not only touched the body, it also impacted hearts.

To this day, Heather is cancer-free.

As I reflected on the way these women embraced my prayer request, I began to notice some parallels between their prayers for Heather, and the prayer request of Christ. The reason these women prayed, and the way they prayed, pointed toward some additional opportunities we have in being an answer through prayer. Not only do we have an opportunity to impact world evangelization, but we also have opportunities relating to the Biblical phrase of faith, hope, and love. Since the Bible says "the greatest of these is love" (1 Cor. 13:13), that's where we'll begin.

## THE OPPORTUNITY TO EXPRESS LOVE

The way people prayed for Heather, especially the women from East Africa, expressed love to me, my wife and others in our family. In sharing that, I'm sure you can also recall a time or times in your life when someone made a strong, active commitment to pray for someone or something important to you. If so, then you've had a chance to experience how good it made you feel in knowing that someone cared enough to devote themselves to pray for your concerns. That's how these Godly women in East Africa made me feel as they prayed for Heather. And we have a similar opportunity in answering the prayer request of Christ.

When you and I ask Christ to send workers, we're expressing love to the Lord by praying about something important to Him .... the harvest of souls. Something so important that He Himself left the glory of heaven, came to earth, and shed His blood so that people could be reconciled to God. By praying this sending prayer, we show the Lord that we care about what He Himself cares for. And, just as the people who prayed for Heather showed love to our family, by praying sending prayers we can show our love for Jesus.

There's a second way that these women expressed love to our family. They did so in the way that they prayed with perseverance. This aspect of perseverance draws another correlation to the prayer request of Christ.

When the Lord made His appeal for prayer, it is recorded, "Therefore, pray earnestly" in the English Standard translation. The New American Standard says to "beseech" the Lord of the harvest.[1] Both appear to be simple phrases, but they actually convey far more. The words "earnestly" and "beseech" represent the need for devoted, persistent prayer: the type of prayer that's represented by one of the definitions for the Greek word for prayer in Christ's request. The word is Deomai, and one way it is defined is with the words "to beg."[2] If we put together the words, "earnestly," "beseech," and "to beg," we get a picture of the strength of Christ's appeal. The Lord is emphasizing the need for you and I to make a difference by being diligent in praying for Him to send workers.

This emphasis on devotion to prayer connects with a principle taught by Jesus in a prayer parable recorded by Luke. It is a passage of Scripture that begins with the statement, "Then Jesus told His disciples a parable to show them that they should always pray and not give up." (Luke 18:1, NIV) This is the way you and I often pray for something that's near and dear to our heart. We pray and don't give up because it's important to us. And when something is important to us, it touches our hearts when others make it important to them and pray in the same way. Therefore, by being diligent in asking Christ to increase the number of harvest workers, we're praying for what Jesus cares about. In doing so, we're showing Him our love.

## "IF YOU LOVE ME..."

When I first learned how important it was to pray this prayer of sending, I have to admit I was somewhat resistant. I believed in praying for those without Christ, and still do more than ever, but when I learned about the need to pray for workers, I wasn't very excited. Perhaps it's because it was new to me, and I didn't fully understand the magnitude of its importance. Whatever the reason, I didn't immediately embrace this prayer. Perhaps you find yourself in a similar place. Maybe you question your desire to pray for workers. Maybe it's the first time you've heard about it and in the newness it hasn't quite "sunk in" yet. Maybe you've been praying for workers for years and are sensing a little "dryness," like it's becoming a routine. Regardless of where you find yourself and regardless of how you're feeling, the starting point and the enduring point in being an answer, is simply a matter of obedience. The good news is that obedience, regardless of our feelings, is an opportunity for expressing love to Jesus.

When Christ gave His request, His disciples at the time wouldn't have viewed it as a request. The way Jesus asked for prayer, and the reason why He asked, would have been clearly recognized as a command. To obey Him would be the normal duty and call for a disciple of Christ. This adds a third way we can express our love to Christ – by praying for Him to send workers. We show it by praying for what He cares about, we show it by praying with devotion and diligence, and we show it by our obedience. By remaining faithful in prayer no matter how we feel. That's because love and obedience go hand in hand.

Jesus said, "If you love Me, you will obey what I command." (John 14:15, NIV) The Apostle John wrote, "This is love for God: to obey His commands. And His commands are not burdensome." (1 John 5:3, NIV) Love and obedience are related. When John drew the connection between love and obedience, he informed us that the commands of Christ are not designed as a burden. His words echo what Jesus said while walking the earth, "...My yoke is easy, and My burden is light." (Matt. 11:30, NIV)

The commands of Christ are not the regulations of a tyrannical dictator, but the guidance of a loving Master who desires to give us life and life to the full. For those who trust and follow Christ, the Lord's commands transition from something we have to do, to something we want to do. And though it's our desire to obey Christ's commands, each of us still faces an ongoing struggle to do so. This is due to the continual battle being waged between our sin nature and the Holy Spirit within us (Gal. 5:16-17). So Jesus said, "Watch and pray that you may not enter into temptation. The Spirit indeed is willing, but the flesh is weak." (Mark 14:38) In this case, continue praying for Christ to send workers. Therefore, a disciple of Christ is willing to love their Lord through obedience to His commands. By being an answer and praying for workers, regardless of what's tempting us not to, we have the opportunity to express our love to Jesus.

## FAITH: THE OPPORTUNITY TO PLEASE CHRIST

There's a small phrase in the Book of Ephesians that says, "And find out what pleases the Lord." (Eph. 5:10, NIV) A similar phrase is found earlier in the New Testament, "So we make it our goal to please Him, whether we are at home in the body or away from it." (2 Cor. 5:9, NIV) Pleasing Christ is something we desire as one of His followers. Another growing "want to," instead of a "have to." Our desire to please Him isn't based on a quest to earn His favor, or merit salvation, since salvation is a free gift from God through faith in the person and merits of Christ, period. But just as we seek to please others whom we love, we also want to please Christ whom, "We love because He first loved us," (1 John 4:19) proving so by His death on the cross.

So what is it that pleases the Lord? A more specific question might be, "How does being an answer through prayer provide us the opportunity to please Him?" One way is that praying for Christ to send workers involves faith, and the Bible says that faith pleases God. The writer to the Hebrews shares this in a reverse sort of way. "And without faith it is impossible to please Him, for whoever would draw near to God must believe that He exists and that He rewards those who seek Him." (Heb. 11:6) If apart from faith we can't please God, then the opposite must also be true: that with faith, we do please God. The women from East Africa who prayed for Heather not only showed me love; they certainly impressed me by their faith. Esther from Rwanda prayed until she truly believed God had given her a positive answer. It's what some might term, "praying through." The woman from Tanzania also expressed to me a strong belief in what God would do in Heather's life. Both prayed in faith and faith is an integral part of the prayer request of Christ.

In Chapter Two a reference was made to a writing by Andrew Murray. He assessed that there were two reasons why Christians fail to pray for Christ to send workers into His harvest field. One was in regard to "missing the compassion of Jesus." The second involves faith.

> … We do not live close enough to God, and are not entirely given up to His service and Kingdom, to be capable of the confidence that He will give it (workers) in answer to our prayer. O let us pray for a life so one with Christ, that His compassion may stream into us, and His Spirit be able to assure us that our prayer avails.[3]

Having the faith to pray for Christ to send workers will not only have a kingdom impact, but also becomes our opportunity to please Him.

## A MODEL OF FAITH

The Bible records many examples about the type of faith that pleases God. These include accounts of people whose faith was so impressive that Jesus pointed them out as a model. One of these faith models was a Roman soldier called a centurion. A centurion generally commanded 100 men, and one was keeping watch over Jesus as our Lord was crucified and died.* It was from the ranks of these experienced, proven soldiers that a model for faith emerged. And through this certain centurion, we not only get a picture of great faith, but the type of faith that will help us be devoted to Christ's request.

> When He entered Capernaum, a centurion came forward to Him, appealing to Him, "Lord, my servant is lying paralyzed at home, suffering terribly." And He said to him, "I will come and heal him." But the centurion replied, "Lord, I am not worthy to have You come under my roof, but only say the word, and my servant will be healed. For I too am a man under authority, with soldiers under me. And I say to one, 'Go,' and he goes and to another, 'Come' and he comes, and to my servant, 'Do this, and he does it.' When Jesus heard this, He marveled and said to those who followed Him, "Truly, I tell you, with no one in Israel have I found such faith … And to the centurion Jesus said, "Go; let it be done for you as you

have believed." And the servant was healed at that very moment. (Matt. 8:5-10, 13)

Here was a man that had so much faith in the authority of Jesus and the power of His word, he not only believed that Jesus could heal his servant, he believed Jesus could do so "long-distance." Not only did the man feel inadequate to have Jesus in his home, he also knew it wouldn't be necessary. "Only say the word" was his request and the man expected Jesus to do the impossible. The faith of this man caused Jesus to marvel and hold it up in front of the people as a model for what it means to truly believe – believe first and foremost in who He is as "Lord," and believe in what He as Lord has the authority to carry out. This man's faith not only pleased Jesus, but the basis for his faith enables us to pray for Christ to send workers with confidence.

The centurion believed that if Jesus spoke a word, then whatever He said would happen. In the previous chapter, "If You Pray, They Will Go," the confidence for believing that Christ will indeed send workers if we ask Him is also based on God's Word. On promises laid out in Scriptures such as 1 John 5:14-15. And just like the centurion had total trust in Christ's spoken word, we can have total trust in His written word, which Paul says is "breathed out by God." (2 Tim. 3:16) This is why we can expect to get to heaven and meet someone whom God inspired to go into the harvest in response to our prayers. And our prayers will express our faith in Christ and please Him. Not because we have to, but because we want to, in gratitude for what He's done for us. This is a great opportunity that carries an "inward" type of faith opportunity as well.

## A PERSONAL FAITH OPPORTUNITY

In the previous chapter I shared a story about going to a village in Southern India. I mentioned that this was an answer to a prayer I had prayed many years earlier. I had asked the Lord to send me to a place that had not yet heard about Jesus and recognized the opportunity in that village as an answer to this prayer. Then while riding in the car I inwardly chuckled. This was actually my fifth trip to a nation where many had little to no knowledge about who Christ is, why He came to earth and what He did. For whatever reason, I didn't remember my earlier prayer until the ride into that village.

Although it took close to two decades for me to understand the answers to my prayer, the waiting actually increased my faith. When the answers to our prayers are slow in coming, we either become discouraged and often give up, or we wait for God to answer at the perfect time and place. The latter is one way that praying sending prayers can make an impact on our personal faith.

The verse from Hebrews we looked at earlier tells us how faith pleases God. That alone is a great opportunity and reason for "being an answer." But the verse doesn't stop there. It goes on to state that God "rewards those who seek Him." One of those potential rewards is an increase in our personal faith. When you and I answer the prayer request of Christ, we'll be praying for places and people we may never visit. Unless we know a missionary, or read about something that's happened among the people and places we're praying for, we may never learn how our prayers were answered – at least not in our lifetime. We may have to wait until eternity to learn the "return on our prayer investment." To pray in this way will take faith in God's word and His promises. And if we remain faithful in prayer, even when we're unaware of the results, but trusting God's promises, our personal faith can grow.

There's no question that answered prayers do and will increase our faith. But how much more will our faith please God, and how much more will our personal faith increase, when we ask Christ for things we know are in His will, but won't learn about until heaven? Do we have this kind of faith? Do we have the kind of faith, "to pray and not lose heart?" (Luke 18:1) A man named George Mueller did, and the following story should inspire us to pray and not lose heart or give up, knowing that we too will someday learn the outcome.

## HE KNOWS NOW

George Mueller was a 19th century pastor from Great Britain. He was known as a man of great faith and was used by God to take care of more than 10,000 orphans in his lifetime. The following faith-story of Mueller's doesn't relate to the orphanage, though that in itself is amazing. Instead, it is a story relating to praying for people to come to Christ. A story of praying and not giving up.

George Mueller wrote, "The great point is never to give up until the answer comes. I have been praying for sixty- three years and eight months for one man's conversion. He is not saved yet but he will be. How can it be otherwise ... I am praying." The day came when Mueller's friend received Christ. It did not come until Mueller's casket was lowered in the ground. There near an open grave, this friend gave his heart to God. Prayers of perseverance had won another battle. Mueller's success may be summarized in four powerful words: "He did not quit."[4]

George Mueller never knew the answer to his prayers in his lifetime. I bet he knows now! In the same way, you and I may never know the answer to the way God uses our prayers for Christ to send workers. "But I bet we'll know in eternity." If you're encouraged by that, then the next section helps magnify the way our prayers have a long-lasting impact.

## THE LIFE EXPECTANCY OF PRAYER

Thousands of years ago, God's people lived for four hundred years in slavery and oppression under the Egyptian empire. As things became progressively worse, God began ordering events that would set his people free. Eventually, the Lord appeared to a man named Moses in a bush in the desert. This was the man whom God would send to help lead the people out of their Egyptian bondage and begin their journey to the Promised Land. Prior to God approaching Moses, we read the following in the Bible: "After a long time, the king of Egypt died. The Israelites groaned because of their difficult labor, they cried out; and their cry for help ascended to God because of their difficult labor." (Exod. 2:23, HCSB)

When I read that verse, it makes me think about the way that God uses prayers that were prayed in the past. Undoubtedly God was hearing the prayers of His people who were alive at the time referred to in Exodus. But how many earlier Israelite generations cried out for deliverance as well? Over those four hundred years of bondage, how many people prayed but died without ever seeing the answer to their prayers? Prayers that their children and grandchildren would one day benefit from.

I've wondered similar things in countries I've visited where people have suffered and died under tyrannical regimes. Now that their country enjoys freedom, I wonder how many Christ-followers died in prison for their faith without seeing their prayers give birth to an answer. Answers that arrived in future generations. Their prayers outlived them and in the perfect timing of God, these prayers were eventually answered. If those prayers outlived those who prayed them, is there any reason to believe that prayers to advance the kingdom through the sending of workers wouldn't be able to do the same?

In his book *The Circle Maker*, pastor and author Mark Batterson gives us a beautiful picture of the life expectancy of prayer through the following story of one of the book's characters, "Honi".

> Toward the end of his life, Honi the circle maker was walking down a dirt road when he saw a man planting a carob tree. Always the inquisitive sage, Honi questioned him.
>
> "How long will it take the tree to bear fruit?" The man replied, 'Seventy years." Honi said, "Are you quite sure you will live another seventy years to eat its fruit?" The man replied, "Perhaps not. However when I was born into this world, I found carob trees planted by my father and grandfather. Just as they planted trees for me, I am planting trees for my children and grandchildren so they will be able to eat the fruit of these trees."
>
> This incident led to an insight that changed the way Honi prayed. In a moment of revelation, the circle maker realized that prayer is planting. Each prayer is like a seed that gets planted in the ground. It disappears for a season, but it eventually bears fruit that blesses future generations. In fact, our prayers bear fruit forever.
>
> Even when we die, our prayers don't. Each prayer takes on a life, an eternal life, of its own. I know this because of the moments in my life when the Holy Spirit has reminded me that the prayers of my grandparents are being answered in my life right now. Their prayers outlived them.[5]

There's great inspiration to think that you can be praying for one of the many unreached people groups throughout the world and someday, in response to your cries (along with the cries of others), the Lord sends someone to gather His harvest. Even more motivating is the thought that our prayers will continue making an impact even after we enter eternity, as the Lord sends workers in answer to our life of prayer. And, just like George Mueller now knows about his friend, you'll also know how the Lord used your devotion to praying for workers when you see Jesus face to face.

## HOPE: OUR ULTIMATE OPPORTUNITY

Whenever the Bible speaks about hope, it's a term that's quite different than worldly hope. Worldly hope is more of a "cross your fingers," "I sure hope so," type of attitude. Biblical hope is a promise, a future certainty (Heb. 11:1), and often points toward the beauty and promises of heaven. Where one day we'll no longer have to struggle with sin and its consequences. When we'll no longer have the daily battles within us, around us, and among societies and nations that cause pain and suffering in various forms. It's also the hope of being reunited with loved ones who have died in Christ. And though these and many other things are definite reasons for hope, the essence of Biblical hope is centered on the person of Jesus Christ and our relationship with Him.

Take away Christ and we'd have no hope. Paul points toward this when he wrote in Colossians, "Christ in you, the hope of glory." (Col. 1:27) And since Christ is the reason for our hope, then the greatest hope of heaven itself is the reality of finally being with Jesus and seeing Him as He is. (John 14:3, Phil. 1:23, 1 John 3:2) In a reference to Christ's future coming, the Apostle Paul also writes, "Waiting for our blessed hope, the appearing of the glory of our great God and Savior Jesus Christ." (Titus 2:13) Later in a letter to Timothy, Paul shares about a crown of righteousness granted to all those who love Christ's appearing. (2 Tim. 4:8) Therefore, since Christ is the center of our hope in heaven, He's the center of our hope now. And, as the center of our hope now and for all eternity, then the ultimate blessing and benefit of prayer, is the opportunity to grow closer to our blessed hope – Jesus Christ.

When we embrace Christ as our greatest reward, this enables us to keep praying and not lose heart when we don't know the answer, or the answer is slow in coming. Regardless of the awareness or speed of any answer to our prayers, through prayer we place ourselves in a position to grow in our relationship with Christ.

## "THE GREATEST JOY"

In 2004, the Lord allowed me to fulfill a dream. For years I'd heard and read about the underground house churches in China. Men and women, young and old, who live and worship under the threat of persecution for one reason – they follow Jesus. Through the church I attended at the time, I was able to make a trip to China and worship in some of these churches.

While on the plane I was reading a book titled Simply Jesus by Joseph Stowell. Early in the book, Pastor Stowell described a conversation he had at a dinner with the prominent evangelist Billy Graham.

> The meal was just about finished when I leaned over and asked Billy Graham the question I had hoped to ask him all evening. Martie and I had been seated next to Dr. Graham at a dinner for staff and board of his organization. Billy, eighty at the time, was lucid and interesting.
>
> Wondering what he would say about his highest joys in life, I asked, "Of all your experiences in ministry, what have you enjoyed most?"
>
> Then (thinking I might help him out a little), I quickly added, "Was it your time spent with presidents and heads of state? Or was it—"
>
> Before I could finish my next sentence, Billy swept his hand across the tablecloth, as if to push my suggestions onto the floor.
>
> "None of that," he said. "By far the greatest joy of my life has been my fellowship with Jesus. Hearing Him speak to me, having Him guide me, sensing His presence with me and His power through me. This has been the highest pleasure of my life!"[6]

A few sentences later Dr. Stowell would comment, *"His lifelong experience with Jesus had made its mark, and Billy was satisfied."*[7] In essence, that's the purpose of this chapter. That's the goal of being an answer through prayer. That's our hope ... to be satisfied in Jesus.

Being an answer to Christ's request grants us a dual hope. A double promise. The first hope (promise) is the opportunity to partner with the Lord in making a Kingdom impact as He sends workers in response to our prayers. The second hope (promise), and the ultimate hope is to be able to echo what Dr. Graham said in the excerpt above: "By far the greatest joy of my life has been my fellowship with Jesus."

The Lord once told Abram, (soon to be Abraham) "Do not be afraid, Abram. I am your shield, your very great reward." (Gen. 15:1, NIV) As you and I begin to understand, believe, and embrace the truth that the Lord Himself is also our greatest reward, then we've just discovered the ultimate answer to the question, "Why be an answer?" Since the Lord is our greatest reward when we pray about anything, it deepens our relationship and intimacy with Him. This was the desire of David (Psalm 27:4), as well as Paul. (Phil. 3:8-10) And when we respond in obedience and faith and pray about something that broke the heart of Christ, we grow deeper and deeper into the ultimate reward of knowing Christ Jesus our Lord. Just as our time and conversations with family and friends enable us to get to know them better, our time in prayer will do the same thing in our relationship with Christ – whether the answers to our prayers are yes, no, or wait.

As followers of Christ, we've been given many opportunities. When Jesus gave His prayer request, it opened the door to additional opportunities. Three of these are the chance to grow in faith, hope, and love. As we live as an answer to Christ's request, each of these can grow in our lives. Opportunity is knocking, and Jesus is knocking at our hearts, calling us to embrace this opportunity and experience the joy of being an answer. It all begins by praying, "Dear Lord, we beg You to send more and more workers into Your harvest field."

# Getting Away With Jesus

1. Can you think of a time you had a burden to pray for a need someone had and persisted on a regular basis? What motivated you to do so?

_____

_____

_____

2. Take a moment to read Revelation 5:8-10. How do faith, hope, and love relate to the promises in that passage? How does it relate to the principle that our prayers will be used by God even after our lives are over?

_____

_____

_____

3. How will seeking Christ as our ultimate reward in prayer help us to pray and not lose heart?

_____

_____

_____

# Section Two

# Being an
# Answer
# Through Going

*"All God's giants have been weak men, who did great things for God because they reackoned that God would be with them." Hudson Taylor* [1]

# 5
# A Promised Partnership

If you've read certain books or motivational articles, the name Derek Redmond might be familiar. An inspiring story emerged in his life that's been told through a variety of media, and rightfully so. It's a story of incredible resilience and determination. It's also the story of a relationship between a father and son that provides a lasting memory for those who hear it.

The stage was the 1992 Summer Olympics in Barcelona, Spain. The event was the 400-meter dash. I was sitting in a hotel room in Columbus, Ohio watching a taped replay of what would become a memorable event. Redmond, a runner from Great Britain, was less than 200 meters from the finish line when the unexpected occurred. The hamstring muscle in Redmond's right leg popped, sending him to the track in a combination of physical and emotional pain. The former was the result of an injury. The latter resulted from the reality that Redmond's hope of a gold medal had vanished. Yet amidst the pain and tears, Redmond rose to his feet and began to limp toward the finish line, determined to complete the race. I couldn't believe what I saw next. A man bolted out of the stadium stands and ran up alongside Derek. The man put his arm around the injured track star and helped the young man continue, eventually stepping away near the end so that Derek could cross the finish line on his own. The man who left the stands to assist the injured Olympian was Derek's father Jim. One writer describing the story also commented on the relationship between Derek and his father. *"They were as close as a father and son could be. Inseparable, really. The best of friends. When Derek ran, it was as if his father was running right next to him."*[1]

As we begin the transition from being an answer through prayer, to being an answer by going, I thought that story would help. Especially the phrase, *"… it was as if his father was running right next to him."*[2]

In those words, we see a correlation to the way we're sent by Christ. One that can provide Godly-confidence for you and I to "go." That's because, just as Derek and his father had a strong relationship and partnership when it came to life and athletics, you and I have a stronger relationship and partnership with Christ as He sends us into the harvest. As a result, our sending isn't designed to be a "solo" mission. Jesus would never send you, me, or anyone else for that matter, without going with us Himself – without "running" right next to us.

Therefore, as we take our place at the starting line for this transition, it's important to realize that our "sending" is a moment-by-moment partnership with the Lord of the harvest Himself. A partnership containing numerous promises without which, the Lord wouldn't expect us to go. In this chapter we'll focus on three promises.

As we focus on these promises, it's done from the standpoint of you and I as individuals. However, just as Christ designed the harvest to be a partnership with Him, He's also designed it to be a partnership with other believers – with the church, and with other Christ-followers. Therefore, as we look at how these promises apply to individuals, may they also serve as a guide, and stimulate further thinking for how we can come alongside one another in the Body of Christ, supporting each other as partners in being an answer.

## THE PROMISE OF PRESENCE

One year my wife and I were staying at a hotel with two grandchildren. We decided to spend a couple of evenings at the pool so the kids could enjoy the water. It was a large indoor pool, and there weren't many places where Sebastian and Audrey could stand without the water going over their heads. Knowing that the water was "deep," I went into the pool ahead of them. Once I was standing in the water, I then encouraged them to jump in because they wouldn't be on their own … I was there.

At first they were a little hesitant, but after jumping in the first time, and realizing that I was there to catch them and keep their heads above water, their hesitancy turned to confidence. So much so, that one time I saw my wife get a look of horror on her face and point to a spot behind me. I turned just in time to see three-year old Sebastian jumping into the pool without waiting for me to turn around. He had developed so much confidence in my presence that even though I had my back turned, because he saw me, he jumped. And, not only did he have complete trust in my presence, I would have never asked him or his sister Audrey to jump if I weren't there with them. On the other hand, because I was there, I not only encouraged them to jump, I was also expecting them to trust me, and come into the water.

This is also the way that the Lord has designed the harvest. Christ would never encourage us to "jump," to go where He's sending us, without His presence. On the other hand, because of His presence, He's not only encouraging us to go, He's expecting us to go as well.

The promise of God's presence is a theme that's woven throughout the Bible. Whenever the Lord gave someone a mission, He also promised to go with them. To Joshua, the Lord said, "Just as I was with Moses, so **I will be with you**. I will not leave you or forsake you." (Josh. 1:5) To Gideon God guaranteed, "…Go in this might of yours and save Israel from the hand of Midian; do not I send you?" "And the LORD said to him , 'But **I will be with you**, and you shall strike the Midianites as one man.' " (Judges 6:14, 16) And the prophet Jeremiah was promised, "Do not be afraid of them, for **I am with you** to deliver you, declares the LORD." (Jer. 1:8)

In each of the above lives, as well as others throughout the Biblical record, God's people were often sent into situations that were way above their heads. Missions larger than they were. But missions made possible because they were never sent alone. God promised to be with them. And, by trusting in the promised presence of God, they were able to fulfill their task, and as a result, came to know God in deeper and more intimate ways.

## THE GREAT CO-MISSION

Fast-forward from the Old Testament to the New and the promise of God's presence is highlighted further. After Jesus rose from the dead, and shortly before His return to heaven, Matthew records a portion of Scripture known as the Great Commission. At the conclusion of this passage, we learn that Christ's command to go and make disciples of all nations is an invitation to a partnership – a partnership with Jesus Himself.

> Jesus came and told His disciples, "I have been given complete authority in heaven and on earth. Therefore, go and make disciples of all the nations, baptizing them in the name of Father and the Son and the Holy Spirit. Teach these new disciples to obey all the commands I have given you. And be sure of this; I am with you always, even to the end of the age."
>
> (Matt. 28:18-20, NLT)

In the opening verse, Christ reinforces His authority as Lord. Lord over everything, including, Lord over the harvest. As ruler over the harvest, Christ is the One who designs the blueprint for reaching the world. In the Great Commission, He reveals the blueprint by instructing us about what we're to do: "make disciples," and where we're to do it: in "all nations." Then in the final verse from this passage, the Lord provides great encouragement for you, me, and all of His followers for the past two thousand years when He promised, "I am with you always even to the end of the age." The Message describes it like this… "I'll be with you as you do this, day after day after day, right up to the end of the age."[3] With this promise of Christ's continual presence, the Great Commission actually becomes the Great "Co-mission." By promising to be with us everywhere and at all times, our mission takes the shape of a partnership whereby Jesus not only sends us, He also goes with us, making this a "team effort" with Christ.

Later in the New Testament, this "team effort" emerges again as we're given the title, "God's fellow workers" (1 Cor. 3:9). Therefore, in being an answer through going, we become an "assistant" with Christ in the harvest. Even during those times when we're sitting down one-on-one with a friend to share the gospel, or ministering without the presence and support of another believer, we're never really alone; we always have a partner, someone who's promised to be with us whenever and wherever we go. That makes being an answer part of a Co-mission – which is the reason Jesus is calling you and me to jump.

## THE PROMISE OF POWER

Immediately after the prayer request of Christ, Matthew records the calling and sending of the twelve Apostles. In doing so, we read about a step-by-step progression that eventually leads to the sending of the twelve.

> Therefore pray earnestly to the Lord of the harvest to send out laborers into His harvest. And He called to Him, His twelve disciples **and gave them authority** over unclean spirits, to cast them out, and to heal every disease and affliction... These twelve Jesus sent out ... (Matt. 9:38, 10:1,5)

After the request for prayer came their call to be with Jesus. But then there's one more step that occurs before the Lord sends them on their mission. That step is found in the words "and gave them authority." The reason those words are highlighted in the above passage is because the word authority can also be translated as "power." As Lord of the harvest, Jesus is not only granting us the authority *to go*, He's also giving us the authority *for going*, by providing the resources necessary for the mission. It's not until Jesus empowered the twelve that He sent them. The authority (power) came first. Without Christ's power, they would have never been sent. And neither would we. The spiritual waters are too deep. We'd all be in way over our heads. Which is why just as Christ empowered the twelve, He needs to empower you and me so that we too can be an answer.

Since the initial sending in Matthew this authority, or power, has been elevated. It's gone from a provision that's necessary for a particular moment, to a permanent power that arrived two thousand years ago. One that was sent after Christ was glorified by His resurrection and ascension to the Father's right hand. And this one's here to stay.

## A PERMANENT PROMISE

In traveling to other countries, one thing I've come to expect is the almost-nightly occurrence of temporary power outages. Some are brief, while others may cause the electricity to be off for hours. Depending on what you have planned, this temporary loss of power can become quite disruptive. As a precaution, generators are commonly used, especially during important events. One year, however, while sharing the gospel in Africa, the generator malfunctioned. Since the crowd was large, it was impossible for most of the people to hear the message. We desperately needed some source of power to begin working. Fortunately, a little over twenty minutes later, things were restored. If it weren't, there wasn't anything we could have done.

Thankfully, as followers of Christ, we live at a time in history where God's power isn't here one moment and gone the next. Thankfully, we aren't placed in a position to wait and hope that it returns. Thankfully, the partnership we have with Christ, enabling us to be an answer, not only includes His promised presence but also the promise of His permanent and perfect power. The empowering that the Lord provided during Old Testament times, as well as the power He gave the Apostles in their initial sending, was only a preview of what was to come.

In former days, God's divine resources were given for a certain period, and then they had to be re-given later. Then Jesus came to earth. And while He was here He taught, and promised, that the temporary giving of the Holy Spirit would soon become a permanent one.

> Jesus said: "If you love Me, you will keep My commandments. And I will ask the Father, and He will give you another Helper, to be with you forever, even the Spirit of truth, whom the world cannot receive, because it neither sees Him nor knows Him. You know Him, for He dwells with you and will be in you." (John 14:15-17)

When Jesus shared those words, one of the promises He gave was that once the Holy Spirit came, He would be with us forever. No more givens and re-givens. No more temporary empowering. Now He would remain. Another promise is that the Holy Spirit will not only live with us, He will also live in us, noted in the words *"He dwells with you and will be in you."*

This personal, permanent empowering of the Holy Spirit is critical to the harvest, and to our sending. So vital, that after Jesus gave the Great Commission and told His disciples to "go," into all the world, He later told them to wait. The mission was to be put on hold until they were sent the power for the mission. "I am going to send you what My Father has promised; but stay in the city until you have been clothed with power from on high." (Luke 24:49, NIV)

This "power from on high" was so important, it's what the Lord chose to share in His final words on earth, "But you will receive power when the Holy Spirit has come upon you, and you will be My witnesses in Jerusalem, and in all Judea and Samaria, and to the end of the earth." (Acts 1:8) Again, it's clear that being an answer was not to begin until the promise arrived. Now that the Holy Spirit has arrived, we no longer have to wait.

He's here, and He's here to stay. He's now the permanent companion of every believer from the day of Pentecost (Acts 2) until Christ returns. And it's Christ's design as Lord of the harvest that the harvest plan was to operate in and through the Spirit's power, and not by the strength of any of His followers.

Before looking at one more aspect of our partnership, let's take some time to examine a couple of reasons as to why the Lord knows we'll need His empowering. And why the task He's sending us to do, is one that He's designed as a partnership.

## COLLIDING KINGDOMS

Whenever we go, and wherever we're sent, whether it's down the street, or around the globe, we never go alone. Christ goes with us. One reason He goes with us is that it enables us to grow in our relationship with Him. The Apostle Paul, writing to the church in Ephesus, shared some of his prayers for them, one of which is that they (the Ephesians) would know "the immeasurable greatness of His power toward us who believe." (Eph. 1:19) By being an answer through going, we get to know and experience Christ and His great power in ways that we otherwise wouldn't. Another reason Christ goes with us and empowers us is that our mission is a "wrestling match." Only this match doesn't take place in a human wrestling ring, but squarely in the middle of a spiritual one. (Eph. 6:10-12)

I have a book in my library titled, *The Valley of Vision: A Collection of Puritan Prayers & Devotions*. In a prayer called, "God's Cause," there are a couple of lines that have become among my favorites: "*I appeal to Thee with greatest freedom to set up Thy kingdom in every place where Satan reigns.*"[4] In essence, this is exactly what we're sent to do. This makes it necessary for us to have the presence and power of the Holy Spirit, since our sending sets us on a collision course between two opposing kingdoms. When the Apostle Paul stood trial before King Agrippa at Caesarea, he shared the story on how he (Paul) became a Christian. In doing so, he also mentioned the commissioning that the Lord gave to him.

"...I have appeared to you for this purpose, to appoint you as a servant and witness to the things in which you have seen Me and to those in which I will appear to you, delivering you from your people and from the Gentiles — to whom I am sending you to open their eyes, so that they may turn from darkness to light and from the power of Satan to God, that they may receive forgiveness of sins and a place among those who are sanctified by faith in Me." (Acts 26:16-19)

To go from darkness to light, and from the power (dominion) of Satan to God, isn't something that can be accomplished through a believer's eloquence, wisdom, programs, or strategic planning. It's done through the power of God, and without His power, our efforts would be futile. This is one reason we're given a permanent, powerful Companion to be an answer. But it's not the only reason.

When Jesus sent the early disciples, He didn't hide the fact that the harvest highway wouldn't be a smooth one. Opposition would arise from any number of sources attempting to discourage them and derail their mission. (See Matt. 10:16-39 and Luke 10:10-16) Therefore, they would need His power to endure, to stay the course and finish the race He's sent them, (and us) to run. Jesus often spoke about the rejection, ridicule, and persecution His followers would face. But He also promised that He would have the last word, and that these difficult times wouldn't be "wasted" or overlooked by His watching eyes. In the Sermon on the Mount He taught,

"Blessed are you when people insult you, persecute you and falsely say all kinds of evil against you because of Me. Rejoice and be glad, because great is your reward in heaven, for in the same way they persecuted the prophets who were before you." (Matt. 5:11-12, NIV)

Often, when teaching on evangelism, I ask someone to share a time they were insulted, or worse, for sharing their faith. After the person finishes their story, I usually give them some type of memento to take home with them. This gift is designed to serve as a reminder and encouragement that the negative experience they had in proclaiming Christ hasn't gone unnoticed – that when those challenging moments occurred, Christ took a "trophy" of sorts, and placed it in the room He's preparing for them in heaven. (John 14:1-3) It's a trophy He'll give to them when He sees them face to face.

Can you think about a time you've been insulted or worse? How did it feel at the time? I believe I know the answer. How does it make you feel to know that Christ is placing a reward in heaven for you as a result of your faithfulness? A reward He'll give you someday in eternity. Christ said that difficult times will happen in the harvest, but when they do, we can be certain that Christ will make sure that our labor is not in vain. (1 Cor. 15:58) And that He'll be right there with us.

## THE DAY THAT JESUS STOOD

The very first martyr of the Christian church was a man named Stephen. After delivering a powerful and convicting message to those opposing the message of Christ, Stephen was led out and stoned by a very angry, hostile crowd and that's an understatement. As their rage started to build, Stephen responded in a way that reveals the partnership He shared with the Father, Son, and Holy Spirit at all times, including this frightening time that would end in his death: "But he, full of the Holy Spirit, gazed into heaven and saw the glory of God, and Jesus standing at the right hand of God." (Acts 7:55)

In that verse, we gain a glimpse of the fullness of our partnership. First we see the active role of the Holy Spirit, filling Christ's faithful servant, causing him to "look up." When Stephen did, he saw Jesus who was now "standing" at the right hand of God.*

A lot more can be discovered from that verse as well as this entire portion of Scripture. (Acts 7:54-8:4) But for our purposes in this chapter, we'll stick to the way Stephen received a clear, "complete dose,"* of the power and partnership he had with Christ in the Great Co-mission. At the most critical of times, the Holy Spirit filled Stephen with the divine enabling that he needed. In doing so, the Spirit pointed Stephen's eyes heavenward where he saw the Lord Jesus standing, providing him with strength and encouragement, while also preparing to receive Stephen and welcome him home to heaven.

From the earliest days of the church, the Lord revealed how He would be with us at any and all times, providing us with whatever we'll need at each specific moment. And, moment by moment, regardless of what we're facing, there's another thing Christ does, and will continue to do throughout our lives. Whether we're sleeping, or facing challenging moments, there's a continual ministry that Christ maintains at the Father's right hand. And this truth is another reason we can have the Godly-confidence to answer by going.

*In the verse from Acts we see the fullness and greatness of our partnership as the Father, Son, and Holy Spirit are all referenced. (The Father as indicated by phrase, "the right hand of God.")

## THE PROMISE OF PRAYER

As our companion in the harvest, one of the most powerful and inspiring things that Jesus does is to pray for us. Jesus and prayer are synonymous.

When Jesus was on earth, He prayed and prayed a lot. He spent nights in prayer, He prayed before meals, He prayed before calling the twelve apostles, and He prayed on the cross, "Father forgive them, for they don't know what they're doing." (Luke 23:34, NIV) He prayed over his followers before going back to heaven, and now that He's returned to heaven, and is seated (or often standing) at the "right hand of the Father," a position of authority, He's actively praying for you and me. Two verses point this out.

> Who is to condemn? Christ Jesus is the One who died—more than that, who was raised—who is at the right hand of God, who is indeed interceding for us. (Rom. 8:34)

> Consequently, He is able to save to the uttermost those who draw near to God through Him, since He always lives to make intercession for them. (Heb. 7:25)

Do you know someone who prays for you on a regular basis? If so, you know how much of an encouragement they are. Yet, regardless of their dedication, these faithful prayer warriors need a break or two. Not Christ. He "always lives" to intercede for us 24 hours a day, seven days a week. As I'm typing this He's praying for me; as you're reading this He's praying for you. He maintains constant alertness. He doesn't doze off, get sleepy, or yawn, He's always keeping watch, and this includes the times you and I step out in faith as an answer to His prayer request.

## A REAL LIFE EXAMPLE OF A SPIRITUAL REALITY

Things weren't going very well during our trip to East Africa. The city-wide evangelistic festival I was conducting started poorly. The first night was one I'd like to forget, and the second night it rained, cancelling our event. With two nights to go and the threat of rain looming in the sky, things looked bleak again. Fortunately, on the next to last night the rains subsided, and the time came for me to climb the steps onto the platform and deliver the gospel message.

As I stood before the crowd, I looked straight ahead and there standing directly in front of me was my friend, Pastor Augustine Butera, who lives in a neighboring country. He had e-mailed me a couple of months earlier, telling me he wanted to attend this festival. He had a strong burden to join me for one purpose ... he wanted to pray. Later I learned that he had stayed up the second night, the night after it had rained and prayed. He stayed awake crying out to God while I slept. Now, as I looked into the crowd, he made eye contact with me and grinned. My friend had positioned himself straight in front of me, about fifty yards away to let me know that he was there. And knowing who he is, I knew he'd be standing there praying while I preached the gospel.

There's a quiet, yet confident sense of power when you know you're not alone. When you know that someone is engaging in the spiritual battle of prayer as you're serving the Lord of the harvest. But my friend wasn't the only one involved in the battle. Jesus was there too, and He was praying. I couldn't see Him, but that's the promise He gave me (and you) in Matthew, "I am with you always." It's the promise He gave us regarding prayer. And, even if my friend would not have been there in the crowd, Christ was still there. He's promised to be with me, and promised to be with you wherever we go as an answer to His request. So while my friend prayed as I shared the gospel, Jesus was praying too. I'm sure this is why we experience a sense of His presence as we enter the harvest. I'm sure this is why we're filled with joy and our intimacy with Jesus deepens as the Lord works in us, through us, and all around us with His grace and power.

Imagine the Godly-confidence that you'd have if you could see Jesus, standing, sitting, or kneeling in prayer right next to you as you ministered to others. I know how confident I felt when I saw my friend standing in the crowd. Imagine the encouragement you and I would have to be an answer if we could see Christ too. And, though we can't see Him, He's still there! Praying, with all His authority, equipping you and me to do what He's sent us to do.

The next time you go to share Christ with a classmate, Christ is there with you. And He's praying. The next time you go to your neighbor, Christ is right by your side ... and He's praying. When you just get off the plane in that foreign country and you're wondering why you signed up with your church for this mission trip, Christ is standing with you at the baggage claim .... praying. When you move overseas to a place where friends are few and danger is imminent, Christ is standing at your beside while you sleep, interceding for you in ways you might not have thought of. It's all a part of the harvest partnership. The Great Co-mission, a ministry we share with Christ.

## IT IS WRITTEN

Jesus is Lord! We've been given His permission, invitation, and command to be an answer by going. He's also partnering with us by giving us His Holy Spirit the day we trusted Christ (Acts 2:38, 11:17). Therefore, He can promise to go with us on a Co-mission, praying for us every step of the way. At times, we may sense a special prompting, conviction, or leading as Christ compels us into the harvest. Those feelings are great, but they are not a prerequisite for being an answer. The Holy Spirit's guidance, direction and timing shouldn't be negated, nor should Godly wisdom and prayer. But we don't have to wait for something special to occur before going. Christ has already spoken. He's already given us permission to go into all the world. If we fail to obey what's already written, will we really obey when the Spirit brings a special prompting? Oswald Chambers wrote, "There are unemployables in the spiritual domain, spiritually decrepit people, who refuse to do anything unless they are supernaturally inspired. The proof that we are rightly related to God is that we do our best whether we feel inspired or not."[5]

I've seen the Lord work through special promptings, and also through simple obedience to what's already written. The Apostle Paul may have summarized it best when he wrote, "For Christ's love compels us, because we are convinced that one died for all, and therefore all died. And He died for all, that those who live should no longer live for themselves but for Him who died for them and was raised again." (2 Cor. 5:14-15; NIV) Our love for Christ, and what He did by shedding His blood in order to bring us back to God, is the foundation for what compels us. And, while the Spirit does indeed lead, He's also looking for a response. That was the advice given to a young man many years ago. A man who's gone on to become one of the greatest answers to the prayer request of Christ in all the world. Perhaps this is what Jesus is looking for in you and me as well.

## GOD'S LOOKING FOR A RESPONSE

Luis Palau is an international evangelist who's spoken to millions, in multiple countries. His love and faithfulness to Christ and His gospel has resulted in many people trusting Christ as their Lord and Savior. Before entering the ministry full-time, Palau's mother wondered why it was taking her son so long to transition from his banking career to a full-time career in evangelism and church planting. Although what his mother shared with him deals with vocational ministry, it can also relate to each of us as we seek to be an answer in the jobs, schools, neighborhoods, and communities where we're strategically and sovereignly placed by the Lord of the harvest.

> My mother was the one who kept pushing me to go into evangelism. Even though I had a good job at the bank and was the only source of income for our family, she kept encouraging me to go into evangelism and church planting. She was persistent, never raising her voice, but continually pushing me to pursue it. One day I replied to her, "I'm waiting for the call." I've never forgotten her response: "The call, the call," she said. "The call went out 2,000 years ago. The Lord is waiting for the response, not the call!"[6]

We've been invited to a partnership with Christ. And the Lord is waiting for your response – your RSVP, to what He as Lord is expecting us to do ... be an answer to His prayer request. We have the permanent empowering of the Holy Spirit. We also have the promise that as we step out in faith, we never do so alone. This is a divine partnership. Christ is there. He's working and He's praying, enabling us to carry out what He's sending us to do. And in doing so, we'll get to know Him in ways that we may never know Him otherwise.

# Getting Away With Jesus

1. Of the three promises examined in this chapter, which one is the most encouraging to you and why?

_____

_____

_____

2. As a church, how can we follow the example of Jesus and partner with one another in our mission at home, with those we know who minister internationally? How might we do so by....

A) Our presence. (even from a distance to those internationally)

B) Our prayers in a way that they will know.

_____

_____

_____

3. What type of response is the Lord waiting on from you? What is the main obstacle that's holding you back, and what is the faith step necessary in order for you to respond?

_____

_____

_____

**Note on the Great Commission:** *The chapters in this book focus on being sent to those who have yet to trust Christ and be reconciled to God. Though this is our focus, it's not the "end-game" of the commission Christ gave us. We're sent to make disciples and to do so means helping those around us grow and mature in their relationship with Christ...especially those whom the Lord enables us to reach through our going. Therefore, in the "Next Steps" section relating to this chapter, some ideas for being a "disciple-maker" will be addressed.*

# 6
# Just As

I was scheduled to speak at a Christian college during their Missions week. The opportunity brought about a mixture of excitement and apprehension. I wondered if some of the students might look at the topic of missions, and decide to use the twenty-five minute chapel as a chance to get some extra sleep, or to study for an upcoming test. My concern was not a reflection on the student body. Instead it was the likelihood that most of the students weren't headed to an "overseas" mission field. I still hoped to engage them with something I firmly believe in: a perspective and understanding that, even though we may not be missionaries in the true sense of the definition, we all have a mission from God … an important one. Although everyone isn't sent to a foreign country, the Lord is sending each of His followers to strategic places to represent Him. He is sending each of us to be an answer to His prayer request by "going."

Over a decade earlier, at another Christian college, I witnessed a memorable illustration related to how each of us is "sent." My wife and I were attending a graduation ceremony at the college and, during the keynote speaker's message, he asked the graduates to stand when he named their respective degree programs. *"School of Business, stand up,"* he said. *"School of Nursing, stand up … School of Education, stand up.*" He continued until all the students throughout the auditorium had risen to their feet. Then he said the following: "*You see how God works.*"

His point was clear. Here were a number of young adults, heading into different occupational settings with an opportunity to represent Christ. They were being sent to places where divine appointments await- ed because the harvest in business is plentiful … and workers are needed. The harvest in our schools is plentiful and workers are needed. The same can be said for truck drivers, construction workers, housewives etc. For two decades I was a teacher and a coach. That was God's plan for me. As a result, He created me with interests and desires that led me into public education for a certain season of my life. Part of my God-ordained role as an educator was to be an answer to the prayer request of Christ at school. It was the specific field where the Lord sent me.

The same is true for you. You're probably familiar with the following verses: "For by grace you have been saved through faith. And this is not your own doing; it is the gift of God, not a result of works, so that no one may boast." (Eph. 2:8-9) As familiar as those verses are, the one following it is often overlooked. "For we are His workmanship, created in Christ Je- sus for good works which God prepared beforehand, that we should walk in them." (Eph. 2:10) So even if you aren't an official missionary, by defini- tion, you have an official mission that Christ is sending you on. Something He prepared for you even before your date of birth.

It's natural to view the prayer request of Christ as something designed solely for those reaching other nations or unreached people groups. But perhaps it's also time we viewed it in areas closer to home, as well as in our personal life. By saying that, I don't want to negate the necessity of praying for Christ to send workers to places and people around the world so that the gospel can reach to the ends of the earth. I also don't want to give anyone reading this a "loophole" by thinking that it's okay to stay where you're at, content with your "local mission." The Lord is seeking people for other parts of the world and that person He's seeking could be you. What I do hope to communicate is that "sending prayers" aren't restricted to a place on the other side of the world. The need is every- where. Therefore, regardless of our title or location, believers have been sent, and are being sent, by Jesus into various places and vocations around the world as His representatives. There's certainly a unique "sending" for those crossing geographical and cultural boundaries as missionaries. There's also an important sending that has a place in our homes, schools, businesses, neighborhoods, etc. We're all "Ambassadors for Christ" and one of the reasons you have the interests that you do is because the Lord has placed that in your heart. He has the right to call you to something else if He chooses, and for some of you reading this book, that's likely to happen, as it did for me. Then again, Christ may also want to send you to a business, school, hospital, factory, or stay-at-home life that's His precise will and purpose for you. Everyone is being sent; it's something we were created for and something Jesus confirmed both before and after His death and resurrection.

## A COMMON SENDING

Thus far, we've looked at how prayer relates to being sent. Prayers offered by you and me, asking Christ to send and multiply the number of workers in His harvest. Now, we're about to look at another sending prayer. This time, it's a prayer from Christ Himself and instead of a request for workers, it's an expression of His perfect will: a commissioning prayer that opens the door, and empowers you and me to be an answer.

Prior to His arrest, trial and eventual crucifixion Jesus prays what I've seen labeled, "the greatest prayer in the Bible." He prays for Himself, His disciples at that time, as well as for people like you and me, as noted in the following words: "I do not ask for these only, (the disciples with Him at that time) but also for those who will believe in Me through their word." (John 17:20) A portion of this great prayer relates to being sent.

> Sanctify them in the truth; Your word is truth. As You sent Me into the world, so I have sent them into the world. And for their sake I consecrate Myself, that they also may be sanctified in truth. (John 17:17-19)

To be sanctified means to be set apart for the Holy purpose of God, bringing Him glory, and by His grace, becoming more and more like Him. (Rom. 8:29) God's holy purposes pertain to every area of our lives, such as (but not limited to) our marriages, vocations, words, finances and character, as well as our various forms of recreation and entertainment. All things are under His Lordship, "So, whether you eat or drink, or whatever you do, do all to the glory of God." (1 Cor. 10:31) All of life in its entirety is to be centered on Christ and His glory.

"Sandwiched" in the middle of these verses is one specific holy purpose pointed out and prayed for by Jesus – that just as God the Father sent

Jesus into the world, now Jesus is sending you and me into the world. The Lord not only states this in His prayer, He also reinforced it with His disciples in one of His post-resurrection appearances: "Jesus said to them again, `Peace be with you. As the Father has sent Me, even so I am sending you.' " (John 20:21) In both of those verses we learn that "as," (or "just as") the Father sent Jesus into the world, now Jesus – the One with all authority – is sending you and me. We have His permission to go, and what He's granted to us as Lord, can't by nullified by any person or institution. Many have tried and will try. The world is becoming increasingly hostile to those who stand and proclaim Christ as Lord. But even when the odds are against us, "if God is for us, who can be against us?" (Rom. 8:31)

Although Christ is sending us in the same way (authoritatively) that He was sent, there's clearly a difference between His sending and ours. Jesus is the only One who was ever born of a virgin. He is the only one to ever live a perfect, sinless life. He is the Only One qualified to die on the cross as the only acceptable payment for our sins. And only Jesus could rise from the grave as the firstborn from the dead; that's His mission and His alone. Our mission, our sending, is centered around making His name and saving work known in our centers of influence and in other parts of the world. And though our specific mission may differ, the heavenly authorization does not. Not only were we sent for the purpose of making His name and work known among the nations, our sending is one of the outcomes of Christ's sacrificial death.

## THE CROSS: DOORWAY TO OUR SENDING

As Jesus prayed to His Father He said, "And for their sake I consecrate Myself, that they also may be sanctified in truth." (v.19) Shortly after praying those words, Jesus went to the cross to die in our place. In doing so, He was completely set apart and consecrated to God. Through His sacrifice the door was opened for us to receive more than just a free death insurance policy. When Jesus went to the cross, as the ransom payment for our sin, He not only did so to bring us to God, He also died to set us apart for God and His holy purposes.

In no way do I wish to minimize the fact that when Jesus died on the cross He paid the price for our sins. He died so we could be forgiven, reconciled to Almighty God, and guaranteed eternal life. God forbid that we minimize that in any way. God also forbid that we minimize the cross by failing to understand that Jesus died so that before I go to heaven, I could be "sent" into all the world as His representative. Believing in Christ isn't a "box to check" in order to settle our eternal destiny and then get on with our lives. Believing in Christ will give us the desire to *get on with His life* – the life He created us for, and the life He wants to live in and through us. The Apostle Paul reinforces this in one of his letters.

> All this is from God, who through Christ reconciled us to Himself and gave us the ministry of reconciliation; that is, in Christ God was reconciling the world to Himself, not counting their trespasses against them, and entrusting to us the message of reconciliation. Therefore, we are ambassadors for Christ, God making His appeal through us. We implore you on behalf of Christ, be reconciled to God. For our sake He made Him to be sin who knew no sin, so that in Him we might become the righteousness of God. (2 Cor. 5:18-21)

In those verses, there's a before-and-after sequence involved in the words that relate to the issue of reconciliation. First, we are forgiven of our sins and reconciled to God. Then, God gives us a ministry and message of reconciliation. A ministry of bringing a redemptive influence into lives by sharing the good news of God's grace to others. Announcing to people who Jesus is, what He did, and why He did it. As stated earlier, I don't want to minimize the work of Christ in saving us from sin, death, and hell. Instead, my hope and desire is to maximize the cross by helping us recognize, believe, and embrace that Jesus not only died to save us from the wrath of God, He also saved us so that we could be sent, and make His grace known to others.

## YOUR MINISTRY

Shortly after transitioning from education to an international evangelism ministry, I began noticing the way I was sometimes introduced prior to speaking.

"P. J. used to be a school teacher and football coach, but 'now' he's in the ministry" I'd often wonder about that phrase, "...now he's in the *ministry*." Actually, my "ministry" didn't start when I left education. Education "was" my ministry. The classrooms and locker rooms of a high school in Northeast Ohio was the place Christ sent me for seventeen years. That was "my ministry."

# The Prayer Request of Christ                                    P.J. Meduri

At this point, you may be thinking that the speaking introduction is just a normal way that most people would introduce someone who had a "career" change. I understand, BUT ... let's think about this a little. Did Christ send me into the educational arena as an answer to someone's prayer? Could it be that someone prayed that the Lord of the harvest would strategically send someone to the school where I taught? When I was hired in that district, was it more than an answer to my prayer for a job? Without a doubt the Lord answered my prayers for employment, but was He also putting me into a strategic position as an answer to someone else's prayer as well? Was a Christian parent praying for a Christian presence in the school? Was a single mom praying that a follower of Christ might cross paths with their son or daughter who attended the school or played on the football team? Was a believing wife praying for a Christian man on the teaching staff to share the gospel with her unbelieving husband? And this doesn't apply solely to me. Couldn't the same be said of every Christ-following teacher and coach the Lord sent to that district in different buildings, different subjects, and among different sports teams? Many of whom I had the privilege of working alongside of and being inspired by. And couldn't it apply to you as well?

Who might be praying for a loved one that the Lord is going to use you to touch at the office, department store, construction site, or next door? There might be significantly more behind your present occupation than the Lord supplying you with a way to make a living. According to Jesus, prayer goes before the harvest, and, prayer goes before the sending of a worker into the harvest. Imagine the potential kingdom impact that you and I, as well as our churches, could make if we believed this and began seeing ourselves from this perspective. One that recognizes how Christ has sent us to a variety of places and people for whom He has compassion.

A growing number of global missions involves people going to various parts of the world in occupations similar to the ones they could have at home. Teachers are going overseas to serve in schools as an avenue to sharing the good news. The same is true of men and women in business, medicine, and other occupations. In fact, we live in an age where you don't have to be a pastor, evangelist, chaplain, or hold some other type of "religious" title to enter the mission field. You can do so in a variety of ways, especially in areas that are highly unreached. George Verwer, founder of Operation Mobilization, writes the following:

> Modern missionaries may be Bible teachers, evangelists or translators, or they may be doctors, nurses, agriculturalists, ac-

countants, or craft workers. Or they may be mechanics, cooks, secretaries, bookkeepers, electronic engineers, or people who are willing to go anywhere and do anything. They must be prepared to go as learners and servants of Jesus Christ and the national church, being what Patrick Johnstone calls "self-effacing spiritual giants."[1]

Since modern mission agencies are viewing an array of vocations as a way of spreading the gospel in foreign lands, shouldn't we do the same here at home? Wouldn't it be great if we viewed all believers everywhere the same way? From John, in an accounting office in downtown Dayton, Ohio; to Sharon on the nursing staff of a hospital in Dallas, Texas; to Gary driving cross-country for FedEx. Think of the impact we'd make if we saw our vocations the same way as Christ does – as a place He's sent us. What type of transformative effect would take place if all believers, regardless of occupation, viewed themselves in this way? What kind of difference would it make in the way we approached our lives if we truly believed we were carpenters, social workers and stay-at-home moms on a mission? I know of one woman who opened her home to other mothers to come for prayer and fellowship with other Christian women, attempting to reach even more women for Christ. How exciting it would be for the people of God all around the world in every arena of life to begin viewing themselves as someone strategically sent by Christ as part of a worldwide global harvest. When we do, we begin living out our sending and become an answer to the prayer request of Christ. One of the most famous Christians in history did just that, and his impact set captives free physically as well as spiritually.

## AMAZING ADVICE

A former slave trader, captured by the grace of God, eventually wrote what might be the most famous Christian hymn in history. John Newton's "Amazing Grace" is known, loved, and sung by many around the world. Though many know the song, not everyone is aware of the "Amazing Advice" that was given by Pastor Newton to an up-and-coming politician.

One day a young man from the British Parliament named William Wilberforce sought a meeting with Pastor Newton, and according to author John Piper, "Not only did Newton give encouragement to Wilberforce's faith, but he also urged him not to cut himself off from public life."[2]

Relieved, Wilberforce set upon a lifelong mission to pursue abolishing the African slave trade. Perhaps like many of you reading this, I thought that abolishing the slave trade was the consuming passion of this heroic politician, but I was wrong. He was not only sent by the Lord to deal with the injustice of slavery, he was involved in a variety of causes such as ministering to the poor, prison reform, Bible and missionary societies, and even the prevention of cruelty to animals.[3] And he was also sent by the Lord to minister the gospel to those close to him. Piper writes:

> Alongside all his social engagements, he carried on a steady relational ministry, as we might call it, seeking to win his unbelieving colleagues to personal faith in Jesus Christ. Even though he said, "The grand business of (clergymen's) lives should be winning souls from the power of Satan unto God, and compared to it all other pursuits are mean and contemptible," he did not believe that this was the responsibility only of the clergy....He grieved for his longtime unbelieving parliamentary friend Charles Fox and longed, "that I might be the instrument of bringing him to the knowledge of Christ!"[4]

Wilberforce certainly made the most of the place where he was sent. His accomplishments are historical as well as eternal. Just as the Father sent Christ, so Christ sent Wilberforce. And he's sent you too.

## SENT TO WORSHIP

A leader of a campus ministry in another nation shared one of the ways he was preparing graduating students to be a witness for Christ in their workplace. A critical strategy was encouraging students to be exemplary employees. This is certainly vital, since the quality of our work helps to advance the gospel as people see us "walking our talk" in the way we do our jobs. Though this is a critical part of our witness for Christ, it's not the sole basis for being an exemplary employee. Another reason is that our vocations provide us with another way that we can worship Christ.

The classes teachers teach, the x-rays doctors read, the eighteen-wheelers truckers drive, and the clothes that stay-at-home moms wash, are all opportunities to glorify and worship God. This is what the Bible teaches in a couple of passages such as the following:

> And whatever you do, in word or deed, do everything in
> the name of the Lord Jesus, giving thanks to God the Father
> through Him.... Whatever you do, work heartily, as for the
> Lord and not for men, knowing that from the Lord you will
> receive the inheritance as your reward. (Col. 3:17, 23-24)

By approaching our day-to-day activities as something that we not only do for Christ, but also viewing them as a gift from Christ, then a larger kingdom perspective emerges in all facets of our vocations and roles. The following comments not only coincide with the above verses, but also relate to the overall big-picture reality regarding our work. Eric Metaxas, reviewing a book by Hugh Whelchel entitled *How Then Shall We Work?*, says that Whelchel:

> ... came to realize that his daily work "wasn't just an avenue simply to share my faith ... or to create wealth to donate to missions work; it was the very thing through which I could be the salt and light Jesus called me to be. "In fact," Whelchel continues, "my vocational work was part of a larger grand story I was discovering, a story that started in the Garden of Eden and continues when Jesus returns and establishes the new heavens and the new earth."

Metaxas concludes:

> Yes, friends, the Lord gave us work in the Garden before the Fall, meaning work is an integral part of His plan for our good. As author Dorothy Sayers said, "... work is not, primarily, a thing one does to live, but the thing one lives to do. It is, or should be, the full expression of the worker's faculties, the thing in which he finds spiritual, mental, and bodily satisfaction, and the medium in which he offers himself to God."[5]

From the verses in Colossians, as well as the comments above, it's clear that part of our sending, and the "good works" we were created by Christ to do, pertains to worshipping God through the passions, desires, and natural gifts He's given us. (See Exod. 31:1-6, and Exod. 35:30-35)

It's one of the holy purposes for which He has set us apart. It also enables us to have a positive outlook on the job God grants us while we're "paying our dues" as we hope and wait for the job we've always wanted. It can also get us through those disappointing times where we're passed over for a promotion, helping us retain a sense of value and worth. God is in control and He's pleased as we offer Him the work of our hands, regardless of the way anyone else might view it. A big part of our sending is to "work as working for Christ." To offer Him worship in our daily lives and vocations – to honor Him with the gifts and talents he's given us, receiving an inheritance from Christ as a reward. These truths can help provide a "divine spark" into any activity we're placed in, even when things become mundane and monotonous.

Like Wilberforce, the place we work can also be an opportunity for having a positive, transforming impact on the environment where we've been placed. You never know how God might be using you to bring change into a setting or culture as you shine your light for Christ. The value of these two perspectives on Christians and work is very important ... but it isn't the end. In addition, like Wilberforce, as we labor in the workforce, we're also laborers in Christ's harvest field – fields where Christ has strategically sent us, approaching each day with the awareness that we're His representatives.

## SENT TO SHARE GOOD NEWS

As we allow the indwelling life of Christ to redeem all of who we are, including our occupations, the Bible also reminds us, "Therefore, we are ambassadors for Christ, God making His appeal through us." (2 Cor. 5:20)

I was surprised a couple of years ago when a businessman shared that some of the Christians he knew in the business world felt that being an exemplary employee was all they needed to do to be a witness for Christ: to shine a light in the way that they did their jobs. There is no question that "our walk must match our talk," and that being an honest, hard-working person of integrity on the job (or at home and in the community, etc.) brings glory to God; however, it isn't the only reason we've been sent. We're not sent just to be model spouses, parents, workers, neighbors, and friends, any more than Jesus was sent for the sole reason of being be a model person, while never testifying to the truth. As Christ was sent, we're also sent to bring the good news, and as the Bible says, "How beautiful are the feet of those who bring good news." (Rom. 10:15, NIV)

Doing so will require wisdom as well as an understanding of the cost. (More on this in Chapter 9). Our nation is becoming more and more like some of the other nations around the world. One who wishes to silence the name of Christ from the public arena. How will we respond to this in the places where we've been sent? For starters, it will help to remember a couple of things Jesus said. Words He spoke to his disciples as He sent them out in both of the chapters listing His prayer request: "I am sending you out as lambs in the midst of wolves." (Luke 10:3) Therefore, we must "be wise as serpents and innocent as doves." (Matt. 10:16) Also, the challenges we'll face do not mean that Christ has abdicated His authority. It won't always be easy, but when we're sent, it's with the presence, power, and prayers of Christ. Therefore, as we're prayerfully and faithfully looking to be His ambassador, good things can and will happen – like many of the opportunities I had as an educator, including one of the very first ones. A divine appointment that the Lord used to get my attention and open my eyes to what He is capable of doing in the places He sends me.

## GOD HAS A SON?

I left the educational profession twice. The second time led to a ministry of international evangelism. The first occurred eighteen years earlier.

I wasn't a Christ-follower at the time and my decision to switch occupations was an attempt to pursue a lucrative career in sales. I was looking for financial independence. In the process I didn't gain worldly riches but found something far better … "the pearl of great price," Jesus Christ. It was during my sales venture that I began meeting Christian people and through these meetings eventually trusted Christ as my Lord and Savior. God had a plan, but it wasn't to pad my bank account. It was to bring me to Himself, and send me back to education as His ambassador.

My return to the classroom began as a substitute teacher. During this same time I also started taking classes for a Master's degree in Religion. One day, as I went to a local high school to "sub", I took along a textbook from my initial Master's class titled "Introduction to the New Testament." I was hoping to have some free time and get some studying done.

My first class that day was Senior-high Government and when the period ended, the students walked to my desk to turn in their assignments. All of the students but one. One young man was running behind and for good reason. He was an exchange student from Asia and was having trouble understanding things since English wasn't his primary language.

When he finally brought his paper to me, he laid it on the desk and noticed my book on the New Testament. He looked at the book, then stared back at me with an inquisitive look and asked, "What's that?"

"It's a book on the New Testament," I said.

"What's that?" he asked again.

"It's a book about God's Son," I said.

He looked at me and didn't say anything. His expression seemed to verbalize once more not a "What's that," but a "Who's that?"

We didn't have much time since I knew he was running late for his next class, so I gave him a suggestion. "Go to the library," I said. As I began speaking, he pulled out a small notepad and a pen in order to write down what I was saying.

"Go to the library and check out a book called the Bible." He wrote this down.

"When you get the Bible, go to a book in the Bible called the Gospel of John." He kept writing. "Read the gospel of John," I said, "and it will tell you all about God's Son." The way he was writing and the interest he showed made me certain that at some point he'd do what I was suggesting.

As he left the room to get to his next class, (fortunately I was free the following period) I remember walking out of the classroom reflecting on what had just happened. I began wondering about the potential opportunities for sharing Christ that I could have as a teacher. Slowly God was getting my attention for the mission He was leading me toward for a season in my life. Little by little His plan began to unfold and by God's grace for the next sixteen years, I taught in a large public high school, where I had the privilege of leading a Fellowship of Christian Athletes ministry. During that time God opened numerous doors for me to share the gospel with students, three of whom had no idea who Jesus was. I had been sent. Education became my opportunity for worship, to be the best possible teacher and coach I could. It also became my mission field and I have many fond memories of serving the Lord as a teacher and a coach. To this day, I've even had the chance to re-connect with former students and talk about Jesus. If the Lord hadn't adjusted my "sending," I believe I'd still be there continuing to "look on the fields" at school.

Just as Christ was sent, He's now sending us. His prayers for us, and His death and resurrection have opened the way. He's sending us to neighborhoods, communities, grocery stores, law offices, assembly lines and any place where a harvest is plentiful but workers are few. As a result, we have an opportunity to be an answer to the prayer request of Christ, not just by praying, but by going as well. It's not an accident you were created. It's also not an accident that you were created with a plan and purpose in mind: for good works that He prepared in advance for you to do. It might not be as a missionary to the unreached, but there's great joy in heaven over one sinner who repents. That "one" may just be waiting for you to be an answer by actively going. Going right where you live and work each day. Christ has created you, chosen you, and sent you – sent you to do an important, unique, and eternal work. To be an answer to His prayer request in a place where a worker is surely needed.

# Getting Away With Jesus

1. What is the "dream" in your heart regarding what you would really like to be doing? Why do you feel you have that dream?

_____

_____

_____

2. The word "vocation" comes from a Latin word meaning "to call." How can this change the way you view your present circumstances?

_____

_____

_____

3. Where has God placed you? Are there people who don't know Christ in your neighborhood, school, workplace, etc.? Are they on your prayer list, and if not, this would be a good time to include them. (See the Next Steps section relating to Chapter Two.)

_____

_____

_____

# 7
# God So Loved The World

Have you ever heard the following statement: "Why are you doing that, there's plenty of people you can help right here in this country?" If you've ever shown an interest in, or participated in an overseas mission you might have heard something similar.

The above statement reminds me of the following cliché, "Charity begins at home." This philosophy certainly has merits. "Being an answer" begins by making a difference for the glory of God right where we live, regardless of which nation we reside in. But even though charity begins at home, it doesn't end there. Even the comment begins at home refers to a "starting point." Sadly, for many people, it also becomes the ending point. It's a comment that contains seeds of truth … it's just not the whole truth. That is because God's heart and plan is so much larger, as indicated in various Scriptures including one of the best-known verses in the entire Bible: "For God so loved the world, that He gave his only Son, that whoever believes in Him should not perish but have eternal life." (John 3:16)

Although that verse is evangelistic in nature, it also reveals a missions theme. From those words we learn the reason Jesus was "sent" to earth … because God loved the world, indicating that God's heart is for the nations … plural. His interest extends to your nation and beyond – into places and people you and I have never heard of. And, since it's a part of God's heart, and in Christ we've been given a new God-heart, then this love for the world is a part of our hearts too. Jesus has a big-picture perspective when it comes to salvation, and a big-picture perspective for you as well. Not only is this a part of God's heart that He's placed within us; it's also an important purpose behind His blessing.

## AN EXTENDED BLESSING

Early in the Bible we learn that the blessing of God was designed to extend to all nations. Roughly 4,000 years ago, when God called a man named Abram He said,

> "...Go from your country and your kindred and your father's house to the land that I will show you. And I will make of you a great nation, and I will bless you and make your name great, so that you will be a blessing. I will bless those who bless you, and him who dishonors you I will curse, and in you all the families of the earth shall be blessed."
>
> (Gen. 12:1-3)

God blessed Abram so that he would be a blessing to others. A blessing intended to extend to "all families" of the earth. God even changed Abram's name to Abraham. His former name meant "exalted father," his new name (Abraham) means "father of many nations"

This blessing that emerges from Abraham and extends to all people is a blessing of faith. (Gal. 3:6-9) It is not an automatic blessing, but an available blessing accessed by faith in Jesus Christ, the Son of God, who died and rose again. "So that in Christ Jesus the blessing of Abraham might come to the Gentiles, so that we might receive the promised Spirit through faith."(Gal. 3:14) The blessing to Abram was not one that began and ended at home. It was to be delivered person to person to person until it makes its way throughout the entire world.

Many years after Abraham, a writer of one of the Psalms understood an important motivation for asking God to grant us His blessing. The Psalmist not only prayed for a blessing upon the nation of Israel, he prayed that this blessing would be given so that the saving power of God would make a worldwide impact.

> May God be gracious to us and bless us and make His face to shine upon us, that Your way may be known on earth, Your saving power among all nations. Let the peoples praise You, O God. Let all the peoples praise You! (Psalm 67:1-3)

There doesn't appear to be any shortage of politicians (regardless of their worldview or party affiliation), bumper stickers, athletes, celebrities, you name it, who use and promote the saying, "God Bless America." But those words aren't designed for the purpose of winning elections, Super Bowls, or Academy awards. Nor is the hope for God's blessing designed as a wish to live in comfort and ease. The Psalmist's motivation for seeking God's blessing was that the saving power of God would be known among the nations and as a result, God would be praised by all people.

Now, many years later, we have received the greatest of God's blessings ... Jesus Christ. As a result our sins are forgiven, our future home is heaven and we have a personal and permanent relationship with God. We now walk through life having the presence of the indwelling Holy Spirit, and each and every moment we can call "Almighty God," our "Abba" Father .... just to name a few of the spiritual blessings we have in Christ. Due to these blessings, God also wants to give us the blessing of making His saving power known through us among all the nations. And though you may never live in a foreign country, if we allow a "home only" perspective to define us, then we'll limit all that God has for us.

## THE WORLD AND CHRIST'S SENDING

In the previous chapter we looked at the way that we're sent "just as" Jesus was sent. (John 17:18, 20:21) Since our sending is similar to Christ's sending, let's look at a passage, written by Isaiah the prophet. This is a portion of Scripture that looks at the sending of Jesus in relation to its far-reaching world-wide purposes.

> And now the LORD says, He who formed me from the womb to be His servant, to bring Jacob back to Him; and that Israel might be gathered to Him – for I am honored in the eyes of the LORD, and my God has become my strength -- He says: "It is too light a thing that you should be My servant to raise up the tribes of Jacob and to bring back the preserved of

Israel; I will make you as a light to the nations, that My salvation may reach to the end of the earth." (Isa. 49:5-6)

In the opening verse, Isaiah points us toward the "base" for the earthly ministry of Christ. It begins with the nation of Israel. Then Isaiah takes it a step further in the following verse, enlarging Christ's ministry to include the ends of the earth: "It's too light" (or too small) of a thing for Christ and His salvation to remain in one location with one nation. The heart of God is for the good news of Christ and His salvation to continue spreading to the very ends of the earth.

Fast-forward from Isaiah, through the life of Christ, to the early years of the church, and the Apostle Paul echoes a similar theme in relation to the gospel. "For I am not ashamed of the gospel, for it is the power of God for salvation to everyone who believes, to the Jew first and also to the Greek." (Rom. 1:16) Once again we see the base of the "gospel operation," the good news about the perfect, miracle-working, resurrected Savior was to be centered on the Jewish people. That was where it was supposed to begin ... not where it was supposed to end. The message of Christ and Him crucified was to go to the "Greek" or the non-Jewish world also. To the "end of the earth," as Isaiah predicted.

From Romans let's skip ahead to the final book of the Bible, the Book of Revelation. There we're introduced to a worship scene that shows that the gospel is not only intended to reach all nations, it's going to reach all nations and in a microscopic way. Not only will the gospel reach countries and cities, it will reach specific sub-groups of people so that all the world will hear.

> "And they sang a new song, saying, 'Worthy are You to take the scroll and to open its seals, for You were slain, and by Your blood You ransomed people for God from every tribe and language and people and nation, and You have made them a kingdom and priests to our God, and they shall reign on the earth.' "
> (Rev. 5:9-10)

So how does all this relate to us? How does the sending of Jesus predicted in Isaiah, and eventually reaching its destined successful conclusion in the Book of Revelation, relate to you, me, and our sending? A return to the words of Jesus help us make the connection.

## JUST AS: PART TWO

When we looked at being sent in the previous chapter, we made note of something Jesus prayed prior to His arrest. "As You sent me into the world, so I have sent them into the world." (John 17:18) He also repeated similar words in a post-resurrection appearance to His disciples. "As the Father has sent me, even so I am sending you." (John 20:21) Once again the word "as," (or the words "just as") are key to examining the world-wide perspective in relation to our sending.

Isaiah recorded Jesus' sending to the nation of Israel as the Lord's starting point. That's where the gospel ministry was launched. Although it was the starting point, it wasn't His ending point, for which you and I should be very grateful. Jesus began with the Jewish people, but His long-term sights were set on the world. To every specific dwelling place on the face of the earth. Even though Jesus spent most of his earthly ministry in the Galilean region (Northern Palestine), the plan for His salvation to go to the ends of the earth would be the result of Him working through His followers. Therefore, since Jesus was sent with a "big-picture" vision, as He was sent, now He's sending us in similar fashion. This indicates that our sending will have a starting point, just as Jesus' did. And it will also include a larger purpose. This purpose is not going to look the same for everyone. Some people will be sent to live in another nation, for one, two, three years or even life. Others will periodically travel back and forth from nation to nation. Others may never travel, but will touch the world in different but significant roles.

Whatever role God has created us for, the new God-hearts we were given the day we trusted Christ, are designed to see the name of Christ honored among all nations. Like Jesus, our sending begins with our ministry base. The places we live. Our homes, schools, jobs, neighborhood, communities etc. This is our starting point. However, since you and I have been sent in the same way Jesus was, our base might be our starting point and primary focus, but it isn't our ending point, nor our only focus. The Lord is seeking to enlarge our vision because there's another part of the world He wants to touch through you and me.

## COMMON WORLD-SENDING ROLES

Though each of us has a different role in advancing the gospel to all nations, there are two common roles in which we can all participate. The first one, we've looked at rather extensively in Section One and it's the role of prayer. Since the harvest progression begins with prayer, our prayers become the catalyst for Christ's sending. And though our prayers start the sending process, there's a second, very crucial ministry in which we can also participate. This role involves our financial giving.

In Chapter Two we addressed some ways to place our hearts before Christ, and asking Him to enlarge our compassion for the lost. We could actually place this section in that chapter as well because Jesus said, "For where your treasure is, there your heart will be also." (Matt. 6:21) Randy Alcorn writes:

> As surely as the compass needle follows north, your heart will follow your treasure. Money leads; hearts follow . . . I've heard people say, "I want more of a heart for missions." I always respond, "Jesus tells you exactly how to get it. Put your money in missions—and in your church and the poor—and your heart will follow."
>
> Do you wish you cared more about eternal things? Then reallocate some of your money, maybe most of your money, from temporal things to eternal things. Watch what happens.[1]

Giving will impact our hearts and increase our compassion. Giving will also help to advance the gospel, enabling you and I to minister from a larger Kingdom perspective. Missionaries from any nation need funds in order to go and to do the ministry. In fact, the principle of people financing the gospel ministry is found in the earliest pages of the New Testament, beginning with the ministry of Jesus.

> After this, Jesus traveled about from one town and village to another, proclaiming the good news of the kingdom of God. The twelve were with Him, and also some women who had been cured of evil spirits and diseases; Mary (called Magdalene) from whom seven demons had come out; Joanna the wife of Chuza, the manager of Herod's household; Susanna and many others. These women were helping to support them out of their own means. (Luke 8:1-3, NIV)

Why would Jesus need financial support during His earthly ministry? Doesn't He own the cattle on a thousand hills? Isn't He the one who sent

Peter to get the resources to pay their taxes from the mouth of a fish? With unlimited funds at His divine disposal, why did Jesus need the finances of some of His female followers? Couldn't His earthly ministry have functioned without this first century donor base? Of course it could! So why did these ladies help support the ministry?

One reason is that it reflects the deep gratitude in their hearts for what Christ had done in setting them free from sin, evil spirits, and diseases. By giving to the Lord's work we also have an opportunity to show our heartfelt gratitude and, the more we give, the more our hearts will grow in love and gratitude toward Christ. (Matt. 6:21)

Through giving we also make an eternal investment. As I write this it seems as if the airwaves are inundated with advertisements for investments like gold and silver, using the sales pitch, "They don't lose their value over time." In actuality, the only investment that doesn't lose its value over time is the one we make in the Kingdom of God. Giving to Christ doesn't depreciate, provide low-interest returns, or become vulnerable to market downturns. Jesus said, "Do not lay up for yourselves treasures on earth, where moth and rust destroy and where thieves break in and steal, but lay up for yourselves treasures in heaven, where neither moth nor rust destroys and where thieves do not break in and steal." (Matt. 6:19-20) This doesn't mean that you and I can't have a savings account or an investment. It's just that earthly investments have a limited longevity.

It's also important to notice that the verses from Matthew talk about building up treasure in heaven. Jesus didn't say that if you give $1,000 today, you'll get back $2,000 by the end of the week. Giving to the kingdom of God isn't designed as a spiritual casino where you pull a donation lever in order to hit the jackpot. Though God has promised to supply our need, He never promised to supply our greed (I heard that somewhere, so I thought I'd use it). The only promise of a rich return is one that we'll receive in heaven, not in the mail by the end of the week. The beauty of investing in God's Kingdom is that you're "paying it forward." God will eventually give you a great return in eternity for your willingness to lose your life for His sake and the sake of the gospel when it comes to finances. So according to Jesus you actually can "take it with you" by sending it ahead through investing in the work of His kingdom at home, and abroad.

Another reason that Jesus set the stage for supporting the kingdom work of God is that it allowed them (the women from Luke 8), and us to participate in the gospel ministry. When the Apostle Paul wrote to the Philippian church, he thanked them for being his partners in the gospel.

Toward the end of his letter we read, "Yet it was kind of you to share my trouble. And you Philippians yourselves know that in the beginning of the gospel, when I left Macedonia, no church entered into partnership with me in giving and receiving, except you only." (Phil. 4:14-15) Paul recognized that the Philippians were partners with him in the spread of the gospel. And, just as the women who gave to Jesus' ministry were partnering with Him, you and I can partner with Christ and others as we sacrificially give of our blessings to help make Christ known among the nations.

When it comes to a big-picture, reach-the-nations style of giving, one of the stories I'll always remember involves a relatively unknown follower of Christ. Through this man's sacrificial giving, millions of people were exposed to the gospel. He was truly used by God to make a world-wide impact.

## PINTO BEANS FOR JESUS

When I first read the story about a man from North Carolina named F.C. Case, I was humbled to say the least. He lived simply and gave to missions even during the difficult days of the Great Depression. Eventually he set a strategic goal to provide gospel literature to millions. In the Book *"Beyond Imagination, A Simple Plan to Save the World,"* by Dick Eastman, his inspiring story is told, including the following:

> The old man's diet often consisted of little more than a ten-dollar bag of pinto beans, which he said might last him a month. His sole income in his later years came from cutting and chopping wood in the Carolina hills (although he never owned anything as modern as a chain saw) and selling it in nearby towns. Yet this man was responsible for providing printed gospel messages for more than eight million people in scores of countries around the world ...He calculated how many people he could reach with a dollar (at that time one hundred families could be reached!), and he set a personal goal of reaching ten million people with the gospel in his lifetime.
>
> When F.C. Case died in 1976 he was two million short of reaching his goal. But he knew that eight million people had been given access to the Gospel because of his faithfulness.[2]

After reading his story once again, I began wondering how many people Case actually helped to hear the gospel. Suppose out of those eight million tracts, one million people came to Jesus Christ and during their lifetime each of those shared the gospel with five people. Combine those numbers with the eight million tracts Case provided and that's well over ten million people; if you keep doing the math, we see a modern-day evangelistic version of the miracle of the loaves and fishes. All the result of one man's sacrificial giving.

So, how might God be leading you to give, so the nations can be reached for Christ? Is it fasting one lunch per week so the money can advance the gospel to unreached people? Is it one less Christmas present this year? Is it an increase in normal giving so the 10 percent tithe you set apart each paycheck, now becomes 10.5 percent? Heaven alone will reveal the way God took the loaves and fish you've placed in His hands and used it to change lives and change eternities. Somewhere, in some part of the world, as a result of your praying and a result of your giving, a marriage has been saved. A child didn't go hungry. A missionary is planting a church. And someone will someday, maybe even today, close their eyes for the last time on earth and open them in full view of the face of Jesus. All the result of your faithfulness in being an answer from a world-wide perspective.

Now, to borrow a sports cliché, we're going to "elevate our game." We're going to move from our knees and checkbooks to our hands and feet in helping to reach the nations. "..As it is written: "How beautiful are the feet of those who bring good news!" (Rom. 10:15, NIV) So why not allow the beauty of being an answer to include another nation? And the first step could be right here at home.

## GOD DELIVERS

Shortly after Delores and I moved to West Virginia, we stopped at a local donut shop one Sunday on our way to church. (I made sure I saved this illustration for a chapter other than the one on keeping a healthy heart.) As we walked in, we noticed that some of the employees were internationals from Nepal who were attending the local college. I was later told that approximately 400 students from Nepal were enrolled at that college. Since moving to West Virginia I've not only talked to students from Nepal, but also young adults from Pakistan and Turkey, as well as other folks from Ethiopia. Three of those four countries I've never visited, but God has allowed me to share the gospel with these international students right where I live. God has delivered a mission field to the United States and although you may never visit certain countries, if we learn to intentionally view people from other nations as God's way of bringing the mission field to us, the geographical impact we can have firsthand on the kingdom of God can enlarge.

This isn't a new concept; many churches have been intentionally reaching out to international students and people in a variety of ways from teaching English, to helping people get settled in a new environment, to housing exchange students. If we actually constructed a list of potential opportunities, that list might be endless. If your church has an international ministry, what role can you play in helping that ministry? If not, what are some of the ways one can be started? For years there's been a prayer movement for nations in unreached parts of the world called the 10/40 window. Maybe one way God is answering prayers for those nations is by sending many people who were born and raised in those nations to the United States so that they'll have greater opportunities to hear the gospel. As we get to know many of these people, God may also enlarge our hearts for another step of faith: One that will not only lead us to seek out those He's sending into our nation, but one whereby we'll step into another nation ourselves.

## STEPPING UP AND STEPPING OUT

I've heard people say that they have no desire to go to a foreign country to serve the Lord. Not the uproot-your-family, sell-your-home-and move type going, but a short-term going, like a one-week mission trip with their church. These aren't people who would love to go, but aren't able to due to certain circumstances in their lives. These aren't fellow believers with a legitimate physical, family, or vocational reason as to why they can't go. These are folks who just don't want to go. It's this desire not to go, that might just represent the biggest reason to go.

Think about some of the Biblical heroes we celebrate. Their initial reaction to the call of God was "not me." "You got the wrong person for that one, Lord." Whether it's fear, apathy, discomfort, or a long list of personal inadequacies, some of the heroes of the faith initially believed they had a legitimate answer to stay put. Perhaps they believed that their reasons for not going would somehow convince God that His interests would be better served by sending someone else.

Moses thought he wasn't a qualified speaker. Jeremiah thought he was too young. Esther knew her life would be in danger. Jonah disliked (understatement) anyone and anything from Nineveh, and, who can forget Ananias in Acts Chapter 9? The last thing on his "to do" list when he woke up one morning in Damascus was to go and witness to a famous church persecutor by the name of Saul. Like these saints of old, your reason for not going is often a qualifying reason for going. This is not a suggestion for making a prayer-less decision. That would be unwise. It is however, an opportunity for taking a reflective moment to ask yourself a couple of questions. First, are there any valid reasons that you shouldn't go?

Second, are you willing to ask the Lord for two things? The first is a desire to go. The second would be for an opportunity to cross your path so that you can go. (This may include actively seeking for one.) Perhaps the first step is a domestic trip where you serve on a short-term project somewhere in the United States. Then the following year is when you "launch into the deep" and go to a foreign country.

Does God need you to go? I think you know the answer to that.

Do you need you to go? I'm going to vote yes. Here's why.

If your decision not to go is based on your will for staying instead of God's will, then we're going to risk quenching the Holy Spirit, and potentially weaken His influence on our lives. Our response, or lack thereof toward these opportunities can have a deeper effect on our hearts than we might expect. The Bible tells us, "Guard your heart above all else, for it is the source of life." (Prov. 4:23, HCSB) Responding in faith to some of the things that demand greater difficulty and sacrifice can certainly guard our hearts in a way that leads to the fuller life Christ wants us to have. It's also an opportunity to worship. If we willfully avoid challenges and sacrifices in one area (in this case serving in another nation), we may begin avoiding challenges and sacrifices in other areas, all or which the Lord is using to bring us to maturity.

If staying home is also a decision based on "your will be done," instead of "Thy will be done," you can also miss something about the Lord you may never experience or learn by staying put. Something that results as we worship Him through obedience, and something we'll learn about Christ that will make us marvel. (John 5:20)

My vocation is international ministry. I've traveled a lot for twenty years, most of those during my summer vacation months while I was an educator. After traveling for twenty years into multiple countries, I continue to be amazed by God when I travel. Whenever I return from a trip I have some type of God-sighting that enlarges my heart and understanding of who God is. His might, His power, His strength in the midst of my weakness, his "bigness"; the list goes on and on. Sometimes I just shake my head and even laugh as God works and continues to reveal things about me, and things about Him, the latter in ways that are truly astonishing. It's not that He doesn't amaze me at home. He does! Jesus said, "My Father is always at His work to this very day, and I, too, am working." (John 5:17, NIV)

However, I believe the Lord often reveals deeper things about Himself whenever we step out of our comfort zones to worship and serve Him in obedience. Stepping out in ways that are beyond what we feel we're capable of. In this case, traveling to serve Him in another nation. I don't believe I can truly begin to understand how big our God really is without experiencing Him from a larger world-wide perspective. And it's not just the awe I sense in watching Him do big things, it's also the way He orchestrates little things. The way He works out just the right details, at just the right time. The way He did one year in Africa.

## A TWENTY YEAR-OLD DREAM

It was one of the more frustrating projects I've been on. The early days of my first trip to this nation were proving to be a "bust," or so I thought. Fortunately, a colleague of mine arranged for me to spend a day with another group staying in the same guest house where our team was staying. When Saturday rolled around, I joined this group for a day of door-to-door evangelism with a local church. I was placed on a small group with a local pastor and a woman from Canada.

After visiting people and sharing the gospel, we were making our way back to the church and planning to stop at one more home before finishing. That's when we saw a man sitting outside of his small house with another man. We decided to walk over and introduce ourselves. As we made our way toward the home, one of the men immediately got up and left. He didn't introduce himself, say hello, or even wave. He exited like we were carrying a contagious disease and he didn't want to take the chance of being contaminated. The man who remained was the owner of the home and invited us to join him. He brought out a couple of plastic chairs so we could sit down, and once we did we began getting to know each other. During our conversation this man asked us a question.

"I was wondering if you could help me?" he said. He continued, "Twenty years ago, I had a dream. I dreamed that I died and was standing

120

in front of this big house but I couldn't get inside. I looked into the house and saw Jesus, but He wouldn't allow me to enter. He (Jesus) began going through the house and each room represented one of my sins. In one room He pointed out my lying. Another room my stealing, and in another room my adultery." He then shared how he had held onto that dream for twenty years.

"Then there was another dream," he said. I dreamed I saw a woman holding a baby, and I knew the baby was Jesus. I asked his mother if I could hold Him and she told me no. She said I couldn't hold Him "because Jesus is holy and you're not."

When he finished telling us this dream, he wondered if we could help him understand. We proceeded to share the gospel with him and after hearing how Christ had died to pay for his sins and that he could be saved by receiving Jesus by faith, the man trusted in Christ right there in front of his home.

I was in awe. Here was a man who held on to a dream for twenty years and I was given the privilege of meeting him and being part of a team that let him know that Jesus was the answer … and I wasn't even supposed to be with this group when our trip started.

I was so amazed at the man's story and how God had worked that I asked this new brother in Christ if he would permit me to share his story. He looked at me and said, "I will definitely share my story," then looked at the pastor with us and asked, "Can I come and share this at your church tomorrow?" The pastor agreed. I then stepped in and said, "That's great, I encourage you to share your story, but I'd like to know if you'll allow me to share it." He graciously said yes.

The following day I was scheduled to preach in another church and couldn't attend the service where this man was going to share his new faith in Christ. When I returned to the place I was staying for lunch, I saw the woman from Canada and asked her if that man had come to the church and if he had shared his testimony.

"He sure did," she said, "And there's more!" Do you remember the man who was sitting with him in front of his home who left when we began walking toward the door? Well, he was a Muslim and he had been telling this man that Islam could help him with his dream. Right at that moment, as a Muslim man was preparing to talk with him, and, not a second too soon, we came walking in. When we did the Muslim man left and the door was opened for us to share Christ with this man.

I was in awe. Not only did I have the privilege of going around the world to talk with a man who was holding onto a convicting dream for twenty years, but we arrived at the exact moment when he was about to hear about Islam. Twenty years, eight thousand miles, the last home of the day, at the exact time it was needed. I still shake my head.

The Lord told Jeremiah, "Call to me and I will answer you, and will tell you great and hidden things that you have not known." (Jer. 33:3). In stepping out of our comfort zones and "going into all the world" God shows us some of the great and hidden things about Himself that we can't get from a book, or even from a church service as important as they are. We can, however, get a glimpse by answering the call to go. Go at home, and go to a place where we can see and experience the greatness of our God firsthand.

Perhaps you're thinking that it can't be done for a variety of reasons. Maybe it's financial. To help you through that, my mentor used to say, "What God orders, He pays for." Though oftentimes the funds may come in a little later than we'd like, as the saying goes, "God's not often early, but He's never late." Maybe it's another reason. Perhaps it's your age. Jeremiah thought he was too young, and Abraham thought he was too old. I'm sure some of those are valid; others just present you with a two-fold opportunity. One is the chance to view His greatness as He helps you overcome the obstacle(s) keeping you from going. The other is a chance to truly worship, by obeying Him even when it's challenging, difficult or seemingly impossible. That's what the people in the following chapter did, worshipping through their obedience, and as a result were amazed.

# Getting Away With jesus

1. Consider reading a missionary biography as a family, Bible study or small group and discussing that missionary's call to the mission field. How did others help to encourage them during their ministry?

_____

_____

_____

2. Take a few moments to read Acts 13:1-3. How are you and your church seeking for the Holy Spirit to raise up more missionaries from your local body?

_____

_____

_____

3. How can you as an individual, family or small group become involved in the areas noted in this chapter? What are some of the obstacles you're facing and what type of faith step is needed to overcome these obstacles.?

_____

_____

_____

_Visit the Next Steps section related to this chapter and prayerfully fill out the chart pertaining to the three areas we've just looked at. This can be done individually, in relation to your families, or with your church, or small group._

# 8
# Taking the Step

It's amazing what happens in our hearts and lives when we step out in faith, when we leave that proverbial "comfort zone" and allow the Lord to stretch us and reveal things about Himself, and about us – things that we would have never known otherwise. That's what the following people did. They left the "zone," and are happy to share it with you. Their stories are different. Different ages, different genders, different ways in which they responded. Each faced various types of obstacles, from doubts, fears, inadequacies, even a financial challenge or two ... but each went, and each was blessed in doing so. I pray you'll notice a thing or two that you can relate to as you read a little about their mission journeys. And I pray it will enable you to leave the "zone," as well.

## FROM APATHY TO AWE

The Lord used a man at my church to touch my heart and give me a vision for international missions trips.

Years ago, I had absolutely no interest in missionary work. In fact, when our pastor invited missionaries to speak at our church, I wished I had not come that day. I found these talks very boring. Years later, my church was sending volunteers to Mexico for missionary work. During the same period of time, a man I deeply respect told me he was leaving his job to dedicate his life to the mission field. I suddenly became curious and the Lord opened my heart to the needs in other countries. I then let it be known that I was interested in going on one of these trips. When I did go, it changed my life.

My first international mission trip was to India. Prior to going, I battled many thoughts of my inadequacies. While my family was both surprised and apprehensive at first, they were very supportive. I, however, was full of doubts. How could the Creator of the universe use this not so young, inexperienced woman? How could I possibly represent this awesome God and King? I felt like I had nothing to offer. All I had was a great desire to go and a willingness to serve Him. I knew He did not need me. He could have sent anyone. I am grateful that He trusted me, even though I did not fully trust myself. I feel honored and privileged that He gave me the opportunity to serve Him in this way.

Although this trip was a number of years ago, I can still see the bright smiles on the children's faces and the sadness in the eyes of the older women. I still pray for them. With each mission trip, I leave a little of myself behind and take a little of them home with me. I have seen the Lord's work during many of my mission trips. However, on my most recent trip, His work touched me in a very personal way.

A few years ago, I went through chemotherapy for lymphoma. Prior to leaving on my mission trip to Ukraine, I visited my doctor for a checkup. The nurse who took my vitals was not one of the nurses I had met before. When I told her about my upcoming trip, she asked if I was going to talk about Jesus. I told her that the purpose of the trip was to share the gospel. She then asked if I would accept a donation. I was surprised and touched by her thoughtfulness. I was anxious to see what the Lord was going to have me do with this gift.

As soon as I arrived in Ukraine, I began to look for the Lord's direction in how He wanted me to use this money. I was speaking to a women's group all week and was sure one of them would tell me they did not have enough money for heat or food. That never happened.

The week went by and I never saw a special need. The night before we left, we attended a church service. Because the worship was in Russian, I spent that time in prayer. I asked the Lord what He wanted me to do with the money. I did not feel He wanted me to just put it in the offering plate. I was worried because time was running out.

When the worship ended, the pastor held up a picture of a young boy and talked for a few minutes. I asked the interpreter what he had said. She told me the boy had lymphoma and the pastor was asking for donations to help pay for his treatments. "Shocked" does not describe how I felt at that moment. I was so excited and could hardly believe what the Lord had done. He sent money from a lymphoma nurse in the United States through a lymphoma patient (me) to a lymphoma patient in Ukraine. Isn't He amazing?

It was through this trip that I really saw how the Lord brings everything together and how very faithful He is. I keep praying that the Lord has not shut the door for me to go on more mission trips. I tell Him, "Here am I, send me!"

## GOD'S PLAN UNFOLDS

My brother-in-law was planning a summer mission trip to Africa and introduced us to an orphanage. Prior to the trip, we met with the founder of the orphanage, whose passion and vision for reaching the lost and caring for widows and orphans was contagious. This trip was out of my comfort zone, as I had never before been to a developing country. In preparation for the trip, I had to get a series of vaccines and, as a hypochondriac, the threat of yellow fever or malaria was a real concern. I also struggled with knowing what my role would be on this mission trip as I am not a musician, singer, or public speaker.

However, long ago God gave me the passion for the game of soccer and the ability to play and coach. I knew soccer in Africa was equivalent to American football in the U.S. and I had always hoped to use my love of the game to share the Gospel. At the time, I had no idea how God would use this sport and me in the coming years. It was truly a step of faith and I realized by putting aside my insecurities and relying fully on Him that I was right where God wanted me to be.

I have seen God work in many ways. The orphanage has expanded and it now houses 41 orphans who would otherwise be out on the streets. God has provided for their basic physical needs and, through this ministry, they are learning about the love of Christ. Many children have come to know Jesus as their Savior.

Additionally, I have seen God work using the great game of soccer.

We started the Kingdom Cup soccer tournament with only four teams. During our last trip, we doubled the number of teams in the tournament. At the end of final match, we were able to share the Gospel with all the teams and the hundreds of spectators, including some of the local chiefs and elders.

God has also allowed us to conduct soccer clinics where we were able to teach basic soccer skills and share the Gospel to the children in the village.

Finally, I have seen God work in my own life. He has given me the courage to share my faith while not worrying about what others may think! We serve an amazing God!!!

## A FAMILY MAKES THE MOVE

My wife and I united in marriage with the intent of serving the Lord as long-term missionaries. My wife remembers her family hosting missionaries on furlough in their home and loved to hear their stories. At this young age she desired to serve the Lord as a missionary. This passion continued to be fueled through short-term trips to Ecuador and the Dominican Republic as a teenager, as well as through missionary biographies such as those of Gladys Aylward and Mary Slessor.

I came to faith in my early twenties but had no Christian background. Within months the Lord developed in me a desire to share the gospel with others. My wife and I met at a singles group Bible study about eight months after coming to faith. Our first meaningful conversation came up over the brochure table of a visiting missionary speaker. That conversation began our relationship.

After a few short months we grew very close. This caused my wife to pray about whether I was "The One." If not, she needed to break it off. One of her criteria was that I would have to commit my life to the Lord's service. I did not know she was praying for these things at the time, but the week she was fervently praying about this, I was facing a crossroads in a job situation. At this crossroads, I meditated on the question, "What do I want to do with my life?" After considering all of the possibilities, I realized the sole satisfying part of my life was spending time with the Lord in Bible study, and that I wanted to serve him for the rest of my life. I brought this up to my future wife. I told her I wanted to serve God with the rest of my life, and I wanted her to be part of it. We were married with no specific goals, but our general commitment to serve as overseas missionaries was clearly stated in our wedding program.

Before heading to Moody Bible College, my wife and I served at a Christian maternity home for teenage mothers. In the meantime I was being inspired by the biographies of Billy Graham, William Carey, and George Mueller. In a Sunday school class while at Moody, I was challenged by other missionaries with the question, "(Besides the gospel), what do you have to offer the people you will serve?" I immediately changed my major to Applied Linguistics, planning to be a Bible Translator. I was deeply captivated by the statistics related to Bible translation, and the sheer lack of the Scriptures in so many native tongues.

After graduation, the Lord abruptly closed this door, as well as every door to long-term service. Our young boy was diagnosed with a genetic disorder. He required a variety of therapies. He also required special attention in school. It seemed best to us to take on this responsibility first and foremost. My wife worked nights as a nurse and I retrained and became a certified laboratory technician.

Prior to the doors closing on ministry, I had read evangelist Luis Palau's biography. At the end of the book there was information about the Next Generation Alliance (a network of evangelists affiliated with the Luis Palau organization). I sent an e-mail and was invited to a conference, but was unable to go. After that, I didn't hear anything for four years.

While primarily serving the family, I had continued my pursuit of ministry, and kept running into closed doors. I was tired of running into them. One day I mentioned to the Lord, "I'm tired of running into closed doors. If you need me, you know where to find me." Yet the desires of my heart yearned to take the Good News to a foreign land. Only weeks later, I received an e-mail from Next Generation Alliance inviting me to consider short-term trips which included Rwanda and Colombia. After a couple of interviews I was accepted with NGA. Through ministering in both Rwanda and Colombia, the Lord started working on my heart. Over the years I had been so judgmental and resistant to the concept of support raising. It boiled down to an issue of trust. I decided if the Lord wanted me to do this, I would have to trust Him for the funds. Through the experience of raising funds for short-term evangelistic programs, I gained the confidence to raise support for long-term service.

During this time I also began seminary. My first class was Biblical Theology of Missions. I was drawn by two passages: Revelation 5:6-14, and the second was from the Book of Romans: "It has always been my ambition to preach the gospel where Christ was not known, so that I would not be building on someone else's foundation." (Rom. 15:20) I was drawn to those who had never heard the gospel. After considering a variety of options, my wife and I chose an existing missions organization whose primary objective is to initiate church planting movements among the unreached peoples. With the Lord's guiding hand upon us, we were led to minister in India.

Around the time the Lord began to lead towards the unreached, our son no longer qualified for therapy. Since we had already been homeschooling our children for several years, we knew we could continue in an overseas context. But being first-term long-term missionaries, we faced challenges in the areas of fund-raising. Attrition rates for first-termers are staggering, causing apprehension from potential supporters. With only 55-58 percent of committed funding and already a few months past our planned departure date, we made a firm decision.

We made a commitment to be out of our house on a specific date which meant we either had to rent it out or sell it by that date. We felt like Abraham: "By faith Abraham, when called to go to a place he would later receive as an inheritance, obeyed and went, even though he did not know where he was going." (Heb. 11:8) Almost immediately after our solid commitment, one of our donors increased their monthly commitment, which boosted our pledged support to over 70 percent. We were given permission to go to India, and shortly thereafter negotiated a deal with a family in our church to rent the house. After departing for India, the Lord brought our support to 100 percent. As someone once said, "God wants His will accomplished more than we do."

We can trust for Him to carry it out, and consider it a superlative honor to partner and serve in His unfolding plan.

## CONNECTION POINTS

I pray that you'll be able to connect with one, two, or perhaps all of these real-life stories in some particular way. Regardless of whether you identify with a fear, a specific life circumstance, or whether what you've read helps trigger a different barrier you've erected over time, in each case God made a way. From finances, to timing, to not knowing what type of role God was sending them for, the end result was the same. Each was able to "marvel" at what God can, and will do. Perhaps you have a similar story, if so, share it with your church, someone might just need to hear it so that they too can "take the step" and experience Christ in ways they never dreamed possible. There's many more stories God is waiting to write. May you, or someone you know, add their names to the annals of missions. Whether it be from a short-term, or a long-term perspective.

# Getting Away With Jesus

1. Which of the stories do you identify with the most?

_____

_____

_____

2. If you were to write a story to encourage someone to take a step of faith in missions, either short or long-term, what would you say? Use the following as a guide to formulate your thoughts.

a) How did you first become interested in taking a missions trip?

_____

_____

b) What were the major obstacles you faced in moving from conviction to obedience?

_____

_____

c) What did you learn about the Lord as a result of going?

_____

_____

# 9
# Finding Life

While I was reading one day, a very small phrase caught my attention. It's not only memorable; it seems very relevant in our quest to be an answer. The phrase was this …. *"Conviction does not equal obedience."* Those five simple, yet insightful words summarized a disappointing venture by a couple of missionaries who were excited to find a church in a place they thought was unreached with the gospel, and were ready to train the church to reach others in the area. Then came the heartbreaking response. They write about it in the book *T4T*.

…… The conviction of the Spirit had fallen on them. The leader of the group stood up before the congregation and said with tears to the group: "For 60 years we have been disobedient to this call. Today, God has called us to obey!"

My friend and I were ecstatic. We spent time praying with the group before we left. We had cast vision, and they had heard God speak.

A month or two later, I returned to make concrete plans with them about when we would begin to train them and how they would go to new villages with the gospel. But what I didn't know was after we left them, they began to count the cost. They realized that if they began to reach out, it could well result in persecution. On this second visit the group that earlier had come under God's conviction said "no." I was heartbroken. It was then that I realized that *conviction does not equal obedience.* I was seeing a living example of the parable of the two sons – where one son said "yes" but did not go work in the field.[1]

The phrase, conviction does not equal obedience, makes quite an impact, just by itself. Yet so does the paragraph prior when the writer makes his assessment as to why the people declined this chance to be an answer. "They began to count the cost." After doing so, they decided to forego this opportunity.

What happened is not exclusive to those in that story. We too have to count the cost and determine the price we're willing to pay, if we're going to be an answer. An answer who not only prays, but one who also goes, and, to what degree we'll live as that answer. The cost will look different for each of us. For those in the above story, it appeared as if their physical safety might be jeopardized, since the writer alludes to the possibility of persecution. For you and me it could very well be the same, if not now, at a later point in our lives. Or, it could mean losing some of our time, our money, our reputations, friendships, or more. I can't predict the future in regards to the cost I'll be asked to pay, nor can I predict yours or anyone else's …. specifically, that is. I just know that there will be a cost. I also know that Jesus said that if we accept the cost and forge ahead, it's actually a road by which we find true life.

## BIGGEST WINNER

Turn on the television on any given night and you're bound to find a reality show on a channel somewhere. One that seems to garner consistent attention is "The Biggest Loser." The broadcast showcases an attempt by people who are struggling with their weight to shed those unwanted pounds. It's a competition where losing actually leads to winning. The idea of losing in order to win also relates to our call as Christ-followers to count the cost. It's a recurring theme in Scripture, as each of the four gospel writers – Matthew, Mark, Luke and John – were inspired to record the following statement made by Jesus: *"For whoever would save his life will lose it, but whoever loses his life for My sake and the gospel's will save it."* (Mark 8:35) Though each writer puts a unique twist on those words, it's clear that the Lord wanted us to understand this life principle. My initial response to Jesus' words was a negative one. All I could see was the word "lose" and it signified that something of great value would have to be exchanged for something else – and it might hurt. In varying degrees, that is the reality facing us. And the negative perspective I so easily have (perhaps you too) is likely the result of a number of things, such as the following.

One is the normal "me first" gene that lives in my sin nature. That deadly gene is always trying to deceive me into thinking that living in a self-centered, self-protective way is what life is all about. That losing is losing and not winning like the Bible teaches. Therefore, this call to discipleship clashes with that old nature, causing me to minimize the cost and lose as little as possible.

Another reason is that I've lived my entire life in a nation where it doesn't cost very much (at least at the time of this writing) to be a Christian. Unlike the early believers, or many Christ-followers in other parts of the world, living in the Western world (especially the United States) allows me to name the name of Christ and follow Him from a lower cost-counting standard. A standard that's acceptable to the culture, other believers, even some churches, but not one that's accepted by Christ. So when I read that the bar set by Christ is higher than anticipated, my first response is how I might find an alternate, more user-friendly, pragmatic route to discipleship.

Third, due to the above, I've grown to like this present world. There's much to enjoy in the country of the "American Dream." Career opportunities, homes, cars, smart phones, entertainment, and all-you-can-eat restaurants distract me and make it far too easy to set my mind on earthly things instead of things above. (Col. 3:1-3) To count the cost doesn't necessarily mean selling off our technology, moving to a developing nation where persecution is a daily possibility, and giving up the steakhouse for locusts and wild honey (though it may). We can, however, expect the goodness of Christ to bring us to places where we'll have to make sacrificial choices. The kind of decision that involves exchanging something large or small for the sake of Christ and His gospel.

If you look at Christ's "lose to save" words closely, whatever we decide to do will come with a cost. Deciding to lose our life and be an answer will come with a cost. And deciding not to lose our life and be an answer comes with a cost too. We'll lose something by living as an answer, and we'll lose something if we don't. One choice is actually a "winning" choice and eventually gives us life and a permanent and lasting joy. The other choice appears to give life, but it has an expiration date. It ends with this life and has no long-term place in eternity. Answering the call to place our plans, our time, our treasured possessions, even our very lives on that altar of sacrifice, is the only cost that's truly life-saving and eternal. There's a passage in the Book of Hebrews that echoes this very principle as it relates to the life of Moses and a choice he made many years ago to sacrifice.

> By faith Moses, when he was grown up, refused to be called the son of Pharoah's daughter, choosing rather to be mistreated with the people of God than to enjoy the fleeting pleasures of sin. He considered the reproach of Christ greater wealth than the treasures of Egypt, for he was looking for the reward. (Heb. 11:24-26)

Moses knew that saving his life and enjoying what the world had to offer would be "fleeting." It would be "here today and gone tomorrow." He also knew that by losing his life, he would find something more valuable than anything the world promised. Something lasting, something eternal, something that led to him making a series of sacrifices during his life, which led to a great reward. You and I will face similar choices in our lives.

## HUMAN-CENTERED OR GOD-CENTERED

Prior to Jesus' life-saving comments, two of the four gospel writers (Matthew and Mark), inform us of an exchange that took place between Jesus and Peter. In the midst of that exchange Jesus points us toward a central truth. One that's easily missed, and if so, can distract us from being a true disciple of Christ's. Mark records the following:

> And He began to teach them that the Son of Man must suffer many things and be rejected by the elders and the chief priests and the scribes and be killed, and after three days rise again. And He said this plainly. And Peter took Him aside and began to rebuke Him. But turning and seeing His disciples, He rebuked Peter and said, "Get behind me, Satan! For you are

not setting your mind on the things of God, but on the things of man." (Mark 8:31-33)

When Jesus spoke about His approaching death, it wasn't the kind of news Peter and the others expected or wanted to hear. They had a different perspective on the job description for the "Messiah." Their spiritual radar screens weren't on the lookout for a coming King who would suffer and die, even though it was revealed in various Old Testament passages (see Psalm 22 and Isa. 53). Instead, they were hoping for a Messiah that would give them an earthly victory instead of a spiritual one. They wanted the actual Kingdom to come now, not in the future. Peter therefore takes it upon himself to correct his Master, only to learn the hard way that Jesus wasn't the one making the mistake. Rather than correcting Jesus, it was Jesus who had to correct not only Peter, but all those listening at the time, and each of us reading this two thousand years later.

Christ's response to Peter and His message that follows can be summed up like this: the Lord's invitation to life is through the cross, not through comfort and ease. The road to life is an invitation to a cross-life, which is the God-centered way. On the other hand, comfort, ease, and a pragmatic approach to following Christ is man-centered. The cross life comes from above. To seek the non-cross life comes from below. When Jesus said, "Get behind me Satan," here's how He defined that "no-holdsbarred" comment: *"For you are not setting your mind on the things of God, but on the things of man."* (v.33) By saying this, Jesus is making it very clear that man-centered Christ-following is not Christ-following. Instead, it's a temptation from the devil to avoid the perfect will of God. Yet just like the cross of Christ was necessary for a resurrection to occur, following Christ and being an answer will follow a similar pattern. A death to self in small ways and perhaps in big ways, but in doing so it eventually leads to life.

## AN EARLY LESSON

While teaching and coaching I was involved with the Fellowship of Christian Athletes ministry (FCA) at our high school. One year, as a fairly new teacher and a fairly new Christian, some of our FCA students asked me to invite a certain speaker to come to our school. I spoke with him and he agreed. As we began discussing the details of his visit, he suggested that he could come to my social studies classes during the day and discuss First Amendment rights in relation to his topic. During each class he would then invite the students to attend a local church that evening where he would present his entire seminar, as well as the gospel of Christ. Sounded good to me.

The day arrived and our speaker addressed my first period class, which was eleventh grade American History. It didn't take long for word to get out and the school began to "buzz." The speaker's topic had offended many of the students.

As the day wore on, so did the tension and the threats. I heard rumors that some of the students were going to go to the school board. Others were going to come to the church that night to attack the speaker. It was one of my earlier encounters with what's more commonly referred to as "spiritual warfare."

The tension even carried over to the lunchroom during my supervisory duty in the school cafeteria. All of a sudden, while close to 700 teenagers ate their lunches, I noticed the early stages of a potential fight. Two girls at the same table began to argue. All of a sudden one jumped up and began screaming, so I began moving in to keep the peace. I arrived just in time. The girl who had jumped up began to charge toward the girl at the end of the table. Fortunately I was able to reach out and grab her by the jacket. She ran right out of the jacket! In desperation, I reached out with the other hand, grabbed her by the shirt and thought to myself, "Oh, please stop running!" Thankfully, she did. That little episode was indicative of the tension, oppression, darkness, and spiritual dynamic hovering over the school that day.

That evening, approximately 150 students came out to hear the entire presentation of our guest speaker, as well as the gospel of Jesus Christ. It went smoothly. No attacks on the speaker, no issues, just a strong night of solid teaching, a good seminar and the good news of Christ. It was a huge success.

The next day after the speaker left, I remained behind and began facing some negative fallout from our event. I began taking a little heat and it made me uncomfortable. I didn't like it. I had read the words of Jesus about "losing your life" for His sake and the sake of the gospel, but now I was getting a very small taste of the cost, and it wasn't pleasant. I remember being in my classroom during a free period and complaining to God about the difficulty I was experiencing. I think I might have even thrown a piece of chalk at the chalkboard in disgust. (I can't remember for certain but it does add a little drama to the story.) I told the Lord, "Lord if this is what serving You is all about, I don't want to do it." In my own way I was reacting like Peter when I learned that following Jesus wasn't all about ease and victory.

Then, in the still small voice in my heart the message rang out, "This is exactly what serving Me is all about." Decision time. I had heard about the cost, read about it, even experienced it before, but in ways where I was able to walk away and avoid long-term contact with those who might be upset. But now it was a little different. I had a choice to make. At the time I didn't realize it, but I had to make a choice between the things of God and the things of man. I still do; it's just that now, over twenty years later, it doesn't come with as much as a shock as it did back then. Challenge yes, fear yes, but shock no. And if you and I are going to be an answer, if we're going to respond at home and in a larger world perspective, then we have to expect cross-moments like this.

The one I described from my school days is minor compared to what the rest of the world faces. I'm almost embarrassed looking back on it, but it was still difficult. The harvest field of Jesus Christ is not always going to be a place of comfort. Not everyone is going to applaud our witness. As a result, it will take a willingness to lose our life in a number of ways, from negative words, to being ostracized by friends and possibly more. But it's a "life-saving" cost. Even amidst the tension of this attempted outreach at our school, I felt "alive." It was a taste of the presence of God who promised, "And be sure of this: I am with you always, even to the end of the age." (Matt. 28:20, NLT) Through that early cross-life moment, the "full life" of Jesus carried me through and graciously helped me understand that this "is" what serving Christ will sometimes entail.

## CHOOSING LIFE

After Jesus teaches us the necessity of a God-centered perspective, He then lays out the details for what a God-centered, Christ-following, life-saving journey looks like: "… If anyone would come after Me, let him deny himself and take up his cross and follow Me." (Mark 8:34) This life progression begins with four simple words, "Let him deny himself."

For starters, denying ourselves isn't a call to give up our uniqueness. Christ made each of us different. We look different, have different tastes, different personalities and different interests, all of which God wants to use for his glory. When we put our faith in Christ, we became a new creation. The Holy Spirit now lives inside us, desiring to live through us, using our uniqueness to glorify God. The Spirit of God will, however, work in us to make changes in our life as it relates to cleansing the sinful parts of our heart, attitudes, and behavior. But if we're walking in the Spirit, then Jesus is going to work through you. Through your eyes, your personality, and the vocation He's given you a desire to work in so that you can be an answer. Denying self doesn't mean we become a carbon copy of other Christians. It means we seek to be like Christ and follow Him. George Verwer explains,

> God's purpose for your life is not to destroy your personality; instead, He wants to enrich it. Being filled with God's Spirit doesn't mean you can't enjoy a sunset anymore; it doesn't mean you won't get excited about music or pizza; it doesn't mean that you won't fall in love, that your heart won't pound or your eyes pop when that someone special comes into view. But it does mean that a very powerful degree of self-control will come into your life, so that you will be able to sort out the priorities, the difference between your God-given personality and your selfish nature, so that you will be able to say "no" to self and "yes" to Jesus. It took me a long time before I slowly, gradually, began to accept myself as God made me. I had this image of what a really spiritual person should look like—very quiet and yet very powerful—and I just did not fit that image at all. I even went as far as trying to dress in a way that I felt people expected, in a dark suit and tie. But gradually I realized that God could use me as I am.[2]

The goal of self-denial and taking up one's cross is not pathological self-abasement or a martyr complex, but being free to follow the Messiah. Self-denial means letting go of self-determination and replacing it with obedience and dependence on the Messiah.[3] That latter phrase, "dependence on the Messiah" is, for some reason, something I failed to equate with denying self for the majority of my Christian life. Thankfully it was pointed out that "denying self" is also understanding that we really don't have the ability in and of ourselves to do so. To take up our cross, to follow faithfully as a disciple. Not in our own strength. That's where Christ's life within factors in. Apart from Him, we can do nothing. With Him nothing is impossible.

## MISSION POSSIBLE

This whole discussion of the cross, counting the cost, "losing our life to save it" is a little (make that a lot) daunting and intimidating. If it makes you feel any better, you and I are in the same boat, and I'm sure our boat is packed full of Christ-followers who are greatly stretched by this passage of Scripture. The Bible also says that all temptations are common (1 Cor. 10:13). You and I aren't second-class Christians if we find ourselves getting a lump in our throats as we're reading these pages. However, before becoming discouraged, the answer for being a faithful disciple is a life-mission that's very possible.

The Bible says that, "He who did not spare His own Son but gave Him up for us all, how will He not also with Him graciously give us all things?" (Rom. 8:32) God the Father allowed His one and only Son to die in our place while we were still sinners – while we were His enemies (Rom. 5:9-10). Now that we are no longer His enemies, but His children through the blood of Christ, we can expect our Father in all His goodness to graciously supply us with all things. Part of the "all things" includes the grace to help us count the cost, deny ourselves, and follow Him, even into those daunting, difficult moments we'll often face by being an answer.

Jesus is the author or founder of our faith (Heb. 12:2). Salvation and the forgiveness of our sins is a work that Christ and Christ alone does on our behalf. This theme is repeated over and over in verses like the following: "I do not nullify the grace of God, for if righteousness were through the law, then Christ died for no purpose." (Gal. 2:21) Until a person realizes that they can't do anything to earn God's favor and forgiveness on their own, they'll never trust Christ and receive eternal life. Since our life in Christ is the result of faith in what Christ did, then picking up our cross to follow Jesus follows the same pattern. It's something we trust Him to enable us to do. Not only is Jesus the founder of our faith, He is the perfecter (finisher) of our faith. (Heb. 12:2) The Bible says, "I have been crucified with Christ. It is no longer I who live, but Christ lives in me. And the life I now live in the flesh I live by faith in the Son of God, who loved me and gave Himself for me." (Gal. 2:20) And by faith in the "perfecter" of our faith, who lives inside us, we can count the cost and be an answer.

This doesn't mean it will be easy, or without difficulty. What it does mean is that following Christ is "mission possible" because nothing, which includes the cost of discipleship, is impossible with God. (Luke 1:37) Therefore, instead of counting the reasons why we don't believe we can live the cross life, let's trust in the main reason we can: "Christ in you, the hope of glory," (Col. 1:27) and cry out to God for His enabling grace. Faithfully trusting His life working through us to do the impossible.

The same Jesus who shed His blood for me, shed His blood for you. The same Jesus who rose from the dead and lived inside Peter, Paul, other Christ-followers we've heard and read about. Those who've faithfully denied themselves and carried their cross – the same Jesus living in them is the same Jesus living in you. And it's the Lord Jesus, the One with all authority, who will enable us to lose our lives in order to find them.

## "PJ, YOU CAN DO THIS TOO"

In my travels I've met some very inspiring people. Some have faced persecution and jail for their faith. Some live in places where safely following isn't a guarantee. One year I was in a place where people had been recently killed. As I met the host organizer for the ministry I'd be involved with for the week, he shook my hand and thanked me for coming.

As we became acquainted with each other, this humble man began sharing about the violence that had taken place earlier that week. Then he shared a little about his life and ministry and told me that a few years earlier his home had burned down. (Before I left, the man would drive me through part of the city where the same thing had happened to many of Jesus' followers.)

After sharing the story about his home, he looked me square in the eye and with great strength and resolve said, "If they want to burn our homes, if they want to take our lives, we'll do it for the sake of Christ and the gospel." Almost instantly the man sitting next to him on the couch, nodded in agreement.

When I saw the commitment of these two men and heard their willingness to embrace the cross-life, even if it meant their home, possessions and very lives, something happened inside me. At the risk of getting a little "mystical," I sensed a type of "inner touch" that I can't classify as emotional, since it seemed to go much deeper. It was like a touch directly into my will. And it came with a silent type of message that I believe was straight from the Lord Himself. "PJ, you can do this too." I realized then and there that the only reason I could ever do this (because basically I'm a coward who is madly in love with comfort and ease), if the Lord led me into similar circumstances – it would not be because I'm capable, but because He's capable. A Bible verse I recall that related to that moment and message is found in 2nd Timothy. "You then, my child, be strengthened by the grace that is in Christ Jesus." (2 Tim. 2:1) By the grace of Jesus and only by the grace of Jesus could the lover of comfort who's writing this book, take up his cross, and "share in suffering as a good soldier of Christ Jesus," (2 Tim. 2:3), like the men I was speaking to that night. One reason this is so hard to comprehend is because at this moment, you and I most likely aren't in the position where this specific type of grace is needed. If and when the time came, the grace and power of Christ will be available to help us do what we can't do on our own. The Lord supplies the grace for whatever sacrifice we have to make; we only need to reach up with the hand of faith and access it. (Heb. 4:16)

A final word in regard to this topic: I've read of people who have lived under persecution for their faith who initially threw down their cross. Our friend Peter who struggled with "foot-in-mouth" disease eventually denied Jesus prior to the rooster crowing. Often an initial reaction to the cross life is to turn back because it seems too heavy. But just like Peter, they've reconsidered, repented and by the grace of Christ endured their cross, bringing great glory to God. Maybe that's you. Maybe it will be me. But whatever happens initially, by faith we can turn back and by the grace of Christ remain faithful. Jesus knew Peter would fall, but He also said, "But I have prayed for you that your faith may not fail. And when you have turned again, strengthen your brothers." (Luke 22:32) This same Jesus is praying for you and praying for me, and by the strength of His prayers and the power of His grace, we too can live from a God-centered perspective. We too can follow Jesus in a "life-saving" way, and as a result be an answer to the prayer request of Christ.

## LIFE-SAVING MOMENTS

In some countries people are fast forwarded to paying a very steep price. From the moment of salvation the cost for following Jesus can be very high. As I type this, news is coming in almost hourly regarding the terror group ISIS, and their violence against Christians in Iraq. As you sit reading these words, many of our brothers and sisters in Christ sit alone in a prison cell. One is an American citizen, Pastor Saeed Abedini, who has now been suffering in Iran for close to three years. Their only crime is their faith in Jesus. However, for most of us reading this book, the cost of discipleship is probably a lot less dramatic. Regardless of what our individual costs may or may not be, we all have the same path to being a disciple of Jesus. We're all called to lose our lives in some fashion. To lay down a certain aspect of our lives on a regular, even daily basis as it relates to our time, money, relationships, reputations, and a variety of other ways. Each one is an opportunity to count the cost and lose our life so that we can gain the greatest victory: growing in our relationship with Christ.

Luke records Jesus' words on the cost of discipleship like this, "If anyone would come after me, let him deny himself and take up his cross daily and follow Me." (Luke 9:23) "Daily" is the key word in that verse as day by day, even moment by moment we have an opportunity to make a decision to lose our lives in a way that allows us to save it. During these times, the Holy Spirit is shaping our character, and transforming our lives into Christ's image.

Take a moment to review your day today, or yesterday, or the past week. Can you think of a time when you had the chance to deny yourself and lose your life by responding in a way that was in line with Christ's will and not your own? How did it go? Did you choose self and comfort, or Christ and life? Each time we face those types of moments, if we can hit the pause button and recognize that God has actually brought a life-giving opportunity across our path, we can actually save our lives as Christ intended. It's these smaller "life-saving" moments that help us grow and mature in our relationship with Christ and prepare us for future "lifesaving" moments. The following excerpt from the book Brokenness, by Nancy Leigh DeMoss, provides some examples of these smaller moments and how losing is actually a positive thing, as we noted at the beginning of the chapter.

> What does this kind of death mean? It means that we must be willing to die to our own interests, die to our own reputation, die to our own rights, die to our own ways of doing things, die to our own comfort, convenience, hopes, dreams, and aspirations. To "die" means to lay it all down.
>
> To give it all up. To let it go. This may seem difficult, perhaps even unthinkable, to our self-protective, individualistic, rights-oriented mind. But, as Jesus went on to tell His disciples, "He who loves his life will lose it, and he who hates his life in this world will keep it for eternal life."
>
> (John 12:25)

What was Jesus saying? The only way to gain your life is to give it up. The only way to win it is to lose it. We think we are giving up so much by dying. But in reality, it is those who refuse to die who are giving up everything...[4]

The last line is the clincher. Only those who refuse to die (lose) actually lose – which is why we're calling this chapter "Finding Life." The ultimate example of this is Jesus, "... who for the joy that was set before Him endured the cross, despising the shame, and is seated at the right hand of the throne of God." (Heb. 12:2) The Bible also states that Jesus humbled Himself and was obedient to the point of death on a cross and, as a result, now His name is the name above all names, and the One that everyone who ever lived will bow before as Lord to the glory of God the Father. (Phil. 2:5-11) God is always going to have the final word. And even if we have to wait until eternity, there's a far greater gain awaiting us if we count the cost and lose for His sake.

## FINDING TRUE LIFE

One time I was asked to speak on "losing your life to save it." The theme was in relation to the way many missionaries have surrendered their lives to missions, giving up their personal ambitions for the sake of serving Christ in a foreign land, and being blessed by doing so. The premise was that anyone who makes this exchange can actually find meaning, satisfaction and true fulfillment in life, and that's true. But something struck me for the first time as I prepared to speak on that topic. It didn't minimize the idea of finding meaning and purpose by losing our lives for Christ, but I kept thinking of the phrase, "find your life," (which is the word Matthew uses to record these words) as it relates to the cost of discipleship. As I did, the following passage came to mind, and with it the full-blown essence of this life-saving invitation.

For you have died, and your life is hidden with Christ in God. When Christ who is your life appears, then you also will appear with Him in glory. (Col. 3:3-4)

Christ is our life. When Jesus says that we save (or find) our life when we lose it, our greatest gain is a deeper relationship with Christ Himself.

There's no question when we deny ourselves and live for Christ, we find far greater fulfillment and meaning. But fulfillment and meaning aren't our Lord. Jesus is Lord, and there is only one Lord and when we "lose our life" for His sake and the sake of the gospel, what we truly save is a deeper, more intimate relationship with Christ.

The Apostle Paul, who lived a full cross-life wrote,

> "Indeed, I count everything as loss because of the surpassing worth of knowing Christ Jesus my Lord. For His sake I have suffered the loss of all things and count them as rubbish, in order that I may gain Christ ... that I may know Him and the power of His resurrection, and may share His sufferings, becoming like Him in His death." (Phil. 3:8,10)

Paul wanted to know Christ, to be close to Him, and it was through the loss of all things and through sharing in the "cross-life" that he found the ultimate gift of God, Jesus Himself.

## "HOW SMALL THE COST"

As a former school teacher I was impacted in 1999 when tragedy struck Columbine High School in Littleton, Colorado. On that April day thirteen students were murdered by two of their fellow classmates, in a violent act that stunned our nation. One of the girls tragically killed that day was a high school senior by the name of Rachel Scott.

One year later, my wife and I were traveling to West Virginia to visit her family over a long holiday weekend. While driving, I happened to hear the radio broadcast of the service commemorating that terrible day at Columbine High. During the broadcast, I learned about a book that was coming out the following day called *Rachel's Tears*, a story of Rachel's life written by her father, containing many excerpts from Rachel's diary. The next day I went to the bookstore and purchased the book. It was fascinating and I read it in a day.

*Voice of the Martyrs* magazine also had an article that I've kept to this day, highlighting a portion of Rachel's diary and containing a powerful summation by the writer of the article. I share it and this brief story of the little I know about Rachel's life not to be insensitive to the tragedy that occurred that day in Colorado. Nor is it shared to "sensationalize." It's shared as a story of victory, a story of how the cross-life is not without a promise. In fact, when Jesus introduced His approaching death, He also told the disciples that things wouldn't end there; crosses never do. Jesus said, "And three days later rise again." Jesus would die, but it was only the doorway to his exaltation. And because of His victory we can rejoice in what the Bible says: "But thanks be to God, who gives us the victory through our Lord Jesus Christ." (1 Cor. 15:57) May the story of this brave young teen, who's a real hero for Jesus, show us the victory that awaits us all. It has parts of her journal shared by her pastor at her funeral.

"I lost all my friends at school," Rachel wrote on April 20, 1998 exactly one year before she would go to heaven. "Now that I've begun to 'walk my talk,' they make fun of me. I don't even know what I've done. I don't really have to say anything, and they turn me away."

"I have no more personal friends at school," she continued. "But you know what? I am not going to apologize for speaking the name of Jesus. I am not going to justify my faith to them, and I am not going to hide the light that God has put into me. If I have to sacrifice everything, I will. I will take it. If my friends have to become my enemies in order for me to be with my best friend Jesus, then that's fine with me. I always knew being a Christian is having enemies, but I never thought that my 'friends' were going to be those enemies."

Some would say that Rachel Scott found true freedom that day at Columbine High School when she exited earth and entered heaven. But I tell you she had found that freedom long before, when she counted the cost of discipleship, then forged ahead."

"If I have to give up everything, I will."

How small that cost must have seemed when she entered eternity and was welcomed by angels, saints, and even the Son of God Himself. " [5]

What a powerful story of someone willing to embrace Christ and embrace the cost. Of all the things that impacted me in Rachel's diary, the final paragraph, summarizing what she said, is what really grabbed me. First is the opening line, "How small the cost must have seemed." In eternity, those moments where we paid the "life-saving cost" are going to seem so small compared to the glory that will be revealed. (Rom. 8:18)

And of all the glory that will be revealed, that final phrase "when she entered eternity and was welcomed by angels, saints and even the Son of God Himself," is a stunning thought. And a word that I know I need to remember on a regular basis.

Someday you and I will see Jesus too. We'll see him as He really is and when we do, we'll not only be grateful for having paid the cost, I'm sure we'll be thankful to Him for allowing us to do so. In saying that, I don't want to minimize the price any of us might pay. My heart grieves for those who pay the ultimate price, of which many are paying at this moment for living as an answer to His prayer request. There are tears, but those tears will someday be wiped away by the very hand of God Himself. And whatever happens, someday in the Kingdom of God we'll be able to look back and know without a doubt how small the cost for being an answer, really was. By God's grace, may all our convictions lead to obedience.

# Getting Away With Jesus

1. The threat of persecution is one reason conviction doesn't result in obedience. What are some other ways?

_____

_____

_____

2. Have you ever neglected to obey a conviction for something that the Lord gave you? What was the reason? Since God is the God of second chances, how might you take a step of obedience now?

_____

_____

_____

3. What is the most encouraging part of this chapter for you? Why? See the Next Steps section for ways to learn more about those living under persecution and how to help and pray for them.

_____

_____

_____

# Epilogue

It's Monday morning, the day after the church that my wife and I attend recognized "Orphan Sunday," which is a day for remembrance, awareness, and a call to action. We saw a video, heard from an organization on foster care, as well as a testimony from one of the couples in the church. I was once again struck with how much need there is in the world and the reality of Jesus' comments regarding the shortage of workers in the harvest.

I've been struck by this reality many times. One evening I was perusing the internet and viewed a website of a ministry designed to rescue young women from the diabolical sex-trafficking industry. While on that site, I saw a link to another ministry that helps rescue babies in a nation where the government has a one-child-only policy for couples. Only two websites and once again, the words of Jesus become magnified. There will never be a shortage of opportunities for bringing the love of Christ, in word and deed (complete compassion), until Jesus returns. What is your answer? God isn't going to love you any more if you answer His request, and He also isn't going to love you any less if you don't. His love is demonstrated at the cross. "This is how God showed His love among us: He sent His one and only Son into the world that we might live through Him. This is love: not that we loved God, but that He loved us and sent His Son as an atoning sacrifice for our sins." (1 John 4:9-10, NIV) God provided the greatest demonstration of His love when we were His enemies, when we had no interest in Him (Rom. 5:9). Then, after we've repented (a change of mind desiring to turn from our sin and self-led life to a Christ-led life) and trust Christ, relying on Him and Him alone to bring us to God, He's certainly not going to withdraw His love now.

But let's not allow that reality to become a loophole for walking away from the cry of His heart. Let's not forget that His grace (His undeserved mercy) wasn't just a way to be forgiven, but a way to say no to ungodliness and to live for Christ. (Titus 2:11-14) Let's not ignore His prayer request by viewing His love from a small "l" perspective. For His love is designed to purify, to perfect, and to transform us into His image. Therefore, what's the next step for you? That's what I hope the final section of our journey, entitled "Next Steps," will help you discover and act upon.

Being an answer through prayer should be the easy part. Asking Christ to send workers into the harvest is something all of us can do if we choose to take this step of obedience. Chapter Five ended with the story of evangelist Luis Palau and the comments from his mother, "The Lord is waiting for a response." He's waiting for each of us to respond in prayer – to obey the command He's given us to be an answer. By doing so, Christ will touch hearts and lives, compelling people to go, and as a result, eternity will be different. You and I can have a part in that both at home and abroad.

Making out a list of names and praying for people you know can also be a step in becoming a complete answer. An answer that goes, as well as an answer that prays. A step you can take by reaching out right where you live and sharing Christ with those close to you. We can also be looking for opportunities to emerge around us, asking the Lord to give us "eyes to see" what He's doing. Jesus said that He and His Father are always working. (John 5:17) He wants to show you where He's working, because He loves you. Since the Lord is working around us, we're to be "making the most of every opportunity because the days are evil." (Eph. 5:16, NIV). And since He's working around us, He'll be working within us, helping us to embrace these opportunities – which the majority of the time we'll have to initiate.

There will certainly be a cost; there will be times it looks as if we've failed or could have done something different, but God "has your back." And whatever He allows us to experience is a way to keep us growing, learning and developing in Godly character, so that we can become even more fruitful in the days, months, and years ahead. We're always being led in a triumphal procession in Christ, (2 Cor. 2:14) even when it doesn't look like it immediately. The more challenging aspect of being an answer by going, depending on your circumstances, is the type of going whereby you leave your country. Whether it's for a few days, weeks, years, or decades, this part of being an answer is something I hope everyone reading this, who is able to do so, will pursue. Perhaps this is for a future time in your life (which, by the way, is not an endorsement to avoid what the Lord actually has for you now). If it is for a future time, you can certainly begin ministering from a world perspective through praying and giving, allowing God to enlarge your heart for the nations right now. You can be a part of this universal sending until that day God sends you. And by the way, make sure that list of obstacles that emerge in your mind, or that special "feeling" you're waiting for in order to go, is viewed alongside the truth of God's Word. Sometimes just being made aware of serving in another nation, or being presented an opportunity, or having something come to mind on a regular basis, may be the way God is moving on your heart in order to send you. Which leads to a final note.

I've tried to find a place for the following at various points in the book. I've tried to include it in chapters, written numerous paragraphs regarding it, but, after all the back-and-forth, it has landed here. At the end of our journey – which might be ironic, as I hope it will actually help us to begin. What is it? It's one final Greek definition. The definition for the word "send." The Greek word for "send" that Matthew uses in the prayer request of Christ has far more strength than our English word for "send." The word is "Ekballo" and it's a word that also relates to the casting out of a demon or a disease (see Matthew 10:1). The famous nineteenth century preacher Charles Spurgeon stated: *"Pray you therefore the Lord of the harvest that He would thrust out laborers into His harvest."*[1] When I first learned of the strength of this word in relation to the sending of Jesus, I pictured a rocket being sent into space from the launching pad – sent with enough force so that tons and tons of equipment are able to defy the laws of gravity and head toward the heavens.

This picture equates with what the Lord does when we pray. He launches people into the harvest. He moves on hearts with a holy, Godly, and perfect "force," compelling people to go with Him, on a Co-mission into the harvest. And He'll launch you and me in the same way, with all that we need to be an answer. So as we conclude our journey, let's all meet together on the launching pad. Instead of putting on a spacesuit, may we put on the armor of God (Eph. 6:13-18). And let the countdown begin as the Lord prepares to launch His people into His harvest through our prayers. And by worshipful obedience, may we live the rest of lives, as an answer to His prayer request.

# NEXT STEPS

The next few pages will provide some practical steps for being an answer. I pray they will be of use, or that they will be helpful in stimulating some ideas for ways that being an answer will become a normal part of who you are in Christ.

## From Chapter 2: Enlarging Your Hearts

## 22 Day Challenge

They say it takes 21 days to form a habit. We'll add an extra day for good measure. In the next 22 days consider doing the following.

- Make a copy of the prayer guide on the following page and pray each day for the names on your list, as well as the prayers for those who follow Christ.

- Consider having a "teammate(s)" from your church or small group and pray for each other's lists and for one another regarding the prayers for believers.

- If you go to share the gospel with someone on your list, have your teammate pray for you, and then let them know how it went and what the next step may be in reaching out to that person on your list.

If you happen to be a church leader, consider making cards like this and distributing them to everyone in your church. What kind of impact might be made if this type of praying became part of the fabric of your church? (The prayer cards our ministry makes are approximately 3.75 by 8.25.)

# Prayer Guide

| PRAYERS FOR THOSE WITHOUT CHRIST | PRAYERS FOR THOSE WHO FOLLOW CHRIST |
|---|---|
| Names For Prayer | Prayer Partner |

1. _____

2. _____        For Christ's Compassion
                                     (Matt. 9:36)

3. _____

4. _____

5. _____

                                     For Christ to Send Workers
6. _____         (Matt. 9:37-38)

7. _____


That the Spirit Convicts Them        For Open Doors to Share the Gospel
(John 16:7-11)                       (Col. 4:2-3)


That the Father Draws Them           For God to Give us Words
(John 6:44)                          (Eph. 6:19-20)


That the Lord Opens Hearts           For Wisdom in Approaching Others
(Acts 16:14)                         (Col. 4:5-6)

## From Chapter Three: If You Pray, They Will Go

On the following page is a 30 Day Chart. The column on the left is an unreached people group(s). The column on the right is the country where these groups live. Think of the impact you can help make if you pray each day for the Lord to send workers to these places.

The reason these groups are selected is due to the fact they do not have a Bible, nor a copy of the "Jesus" film translated in their language (as listed by the Joshua project). They are not selected due to any bias or preference from the author, but based on their lack of access to gospel resources. There are other groups that will fall into this category, but we are keeping the chart at 30 so it can be utilized each day of the month.

The final two columns on the unreached side have been purposely left blank in order for you to fill it in with a group or nation that you're particularly burdened for. For more information visit www.joshuaproject. net, or download the free app, JP Unreached.

| Unreached People Group | Country |
|---|---|
| 1. Aimag Chad, Nuristani Waigeli | Afghanistan |
| 2. Khinalug, Ketsh Khalkh | Azerbaijan |
| 3. Dakpa, Dzala | Bhutan |
| 4. Dagaari Dioula Wala | Burkina Faso |
| 5. Cham Western | Cambodis |
| 6. Fulani, Bagrimi | Central African Republic |
| 7. Ani | China |
| 8. Nakuk Maku | Colombia |
| 9. Loma | Cote D'Ivoire |
| 10. Argobba | Ethiopia |
| 11. Badyara Badyaranke | Guinea |
| 12. Biafada Biafar | Guinea-Bissau |
| 13. Deori | India |
| 14. Dondo | Indonesia |
| 15. Mandaean | Iran |
| 16. Lamet Khamet | Laos |
| 17. Bedoin Fazzam | Libya |
| 18. Bozo Hain, Idaksahak | Mali |
| 19. Chak | Myanmar |
| 20. Kanuri Tamari | Niger |
| 21. Baangi, Cibaangi | Nigeria |
| 22. Chitrail | Paskistan |
| 23. Tunni | Somalia |
| 24. Yagnob Yagnobi | Tajikstan |
| 25. Lao Ngaew | Thailand |
| 26. Jerba | Tunisia |
| 27. Abaza, Pontic Greek | Turkey |
| 28. Hani, Laha | Vietnam |
| 29. | |
| 30. | |

In addition, can you list some local, state, or national groups to pray for each day as well? Asking Christ to send workers to these groups will make another kingdom impact.

## Chapter Five: A Promised Partnership

As noted in Chapter Five, Christ's Great Commission (Matt. 28:18-20) involves you and I being sent to make disciples. Therefore, let's look at some ideas for doing so, based on the following question.

How were you discipled? In addition to the guidance and teaching you received from a pastor or teacher, was there another person who came alongside you to help you begin growing in your faith? What were some of the things they did to help you? Things like the following:

A) Met with you regularly for the purpose of reading, praying and studying the Bible or some type of Biblically-based discipleship materials?

B) Spent time with you on a more informal basis where you discussed Biblical things in a conversational way? (See Deut. 6:6-7 for a learning principle that can make discipling a normal way of life.)

C) Helped you connect with a local church, Bible study and/ or small group, enabling you to meet other Christ-followers that you developed relationships with? My mentor used to say that if a new believer didn't make 5 to 6 friends in a church within the first six months of their conversion, they'll likely leave that church (Acts 2:42, 1 John 1:3-4).

D) Invited you to serve in a ministry they were involved in?

E) Encouraged you to "be an answer," by encouraging you to share your faith?

Whether or not you can identify a person who did one or more of those things in your life, which of these can you implement in the life of someone else? Whatever it might be, what's most important is that we come alongside others, to give of our time and our presence, especially to those who may have come to Christ as result of our "being an answer." In doing so, we can help them to grow in their faith by...

Seeking God through His word and fellowship with a local body of believers.

Helping them become involved in serving and identifying their gifts.

Encouraging and helping them to be a witness for Christ (to be an answer).

Hopefully what's shared will help provide ideas or stimulate others in the area of making disciples. For additional thoughts see the book, *Multiply* by Francis Chan, as well as the booklet *Born to Reproduce* by Dawson Trotman.

## Chapter Six: Just As

1. By using the sample prayer resource from chapter two (Next Steps), what are some ways you can show the love of Christ to those you placed on this list? Ask God to give you "eyes to see" what you can do and to give you wisdom for bringing the message of Christ to them by...

--your words
--Christian literature or some type of media resource
--inviting them to church or a Christian event
--asking how you can pray for them.

Once you approach these people, depending on their interest and/or response, what will be the next step in reaching out to them?

2. Take some time to visit the following website: thegospelatwork.com for further encouragement in living out your faith where you've been sent.

3. Check with your pastor regarding organizations that can help you use your vocation in short-term missions.

## Chapter Seven: God So Loved The World

Look at the Chart below. If you're already involved in one of these "world-perspectives", fill in the column that says "how," with the specific way you're involved. If you aren't presently involved, write down a step you can take to become so in the column labeled, "A new beginning."

| World-Perspective | How are you involved? | A New Beginning |
|---|---|---|
| Prayer | | |
| Giving | | |
| Going | | |

A missionary was once asked what it was that people could do to help them. They said how encouraging it was to receive a note or an e-mail letting them know you're thinking about and praying for them. Therefore, what are some things you can do as an individual, church, or family to regularly write, encourage, or even send a package of sorts to missionaries you know and/or support?

As a church, are you praying for God to send people into missions from your local church family?

## Chapter Eight: Taking The Step

Talk to a missionary, or someone from your church that's taken a short-term missions trip. Ask them the following questions and see if any of their answers resonate with some of the thoughts you have in relation to "taking a step" yourself.

1. What did The Lord use to touch your heart and give you this vision for an international missions trip?

2. What were some of the early obstacles you faced? Thoughts you had of "why this can't happen"? Were there obstacles from other people?

3. How have you seen The Lord work? What has He revealed to you about Himself that you might not have known had you not stepped out in faith?

## Chapter Nine: Finding Life

One way to help us understand the cost of following Christ would be to subscribe to an e-mail newsletter from one of the following organizations:

Voice of the Martyrs: www.persecution.com

Open Doors USA: www.opendoorsusa.org

This will also allow us to pray for people who right now are living under persecution and even provide a way to write to some of our brothers and sisters in prison for their faith.

## Additional Resources and Recommended Reading

Dr. Daniel L. Akin, *Ten Who Changed the World* (Nashville, Tennessee: B & H Publishing Group, 2012).

Norman Grubb, *Rees Howells: Intercessor* (Fort Washington, PA, 19034: Christian Literature Crusade, 1999).

Kevin G. Harney, *Organic Outreach for Ordinary People: Sharing Good News Naturally* (Grand Rapids, Michigan 49530: Zondervan, 2009).

Jason Mandryk, *Operation World: The Definitive Prayer Guide to Every Nation* (Biblica Publishing 2010, 7th Edition).

Nik Ripken and Greg Lewis, *The Insanity of God: A True Story of Faith Resurrected* (Nashville, Tennessee: B & H Publishing Group, 2013).

Bob and Matthew R. Jacks with Pam Mellskog, *Divine Appointments* (Colorado Springs, CO 80935: NavPress, 2002).

David Sitton, *Reckless Abandon: A Gospel Pioneer's Exploits Among the Most Difficult to Reach Peoples* (Greenville, SC 29609: Ambassador International, Belfast, BT6 8DD, Northern Ireland, UK, 2011, 2013).

## Websites:

*www.desiringgod.org*
A place to find numerous missionary biographies.

*www.thegospelatwork.com*
This site will help provide insight into living a gospel-centered life in the workplace.

*www.gospelmovements.org*
A united effort between churches and local cultural leaders to help meet the needs of their community by showing and sharing the love of Christ.

*Joshua Project: www.joshuaproject.net*
Learn about unreached people groups and how to strategically pray for each. (Their mobile app, JP Unreached, is a free download which provides a different people group to pray for each day.)

# Bibliography

## INTRODUCTION

1. William Fay and Ralph Hodge, *Share Jesus Without Fear* (Nashville, TN: LifeWay Press, 1997), p. 15.

2. Taken from a definition found on the Merriam-Webster online dictionary. http://www.merriam-webster.com/dictionary/request

3. Definitions for "Deomai" found from *Strong's Concordance*, and HELPS Word-Studies, http://www.biblehub.com/greek/1189.htm

## SECTION ONE

1. E.M. Bounds, *The Complete Works Of E. M. Bounds on Prayer.* (Grand Rapids, MI: Baker Book House Company, 1990), p. 146.

## CHAPTER 1

1. Used with permission. For more information on Operation Christmas Child, visit www.samaritans purse.org.

2. Tim Stafford, "Imperfect Instrument: World Vision's Founder Led a Tragic and Inspiring Life." http://www.christianitytoday.com/ct/2005/march/19.56.html, accessed August 25, 2012.

3. Ibid.

4. Taken from the Full Definition of COMPASSION, found on the Merriam-Webster online dictionary. http://www.merriam-webster.com/dictionary/ compassion

5. Joseph H. Thayer, *Thayer's Greek-English Lexicon of the New Testament.* (Peabody, Massachusetts: Hendrickson Publishers, Inc., 2007), p. 584.

6. John MacArthur, *The MacArthur New Testament Commentary; Matthew 8-15.* (Chicago, IL: Moody Publishers, 1987), p. 109.

7. Jonathan Martin, *Giving Wisely: Killing with Kindness or Empowering Lasting Transformation?* (Sisters, Oregon: Last Chapter Publishing LLC, 2008), p. 145.

## CHAPTER 2

1. Andrew Murray, *The Collected Works and Sermons of Reverend Andrew Murray*: Kindle Edition (The Christian Miracle Foundation, 2011), location 16016, 16031.

2. David Platt, "The Fuel of Death-Defying Missions;" Posted on Youtube by Truth Endures from the Together for the Gospel Conference; 2012

3. Oswald Chambers, *If You Will Ask: Reflections on the Power of Prayer.* (Grand Rapids, MI., Discovery House Publishers, 1985 by Chosen Books), p. 7.

4. Andrew Murray, *The Collected Works and Sermons of Reverend Andrew Murray* [Kindle Edition]. (The Christian Miracle Foundation, 2011), location 16046.

5. Used by Permission. *Chain Reaction: A Call to Compassionate Revolution.* Darrell Scott with Steve Rabey, 2001, Thomas Nelson. Nashville, Tennessee. All rights reserved. p. 141

6. Brian Orme, "Compassionate Evangelism: A Few Words with Francis Chan." Interview, *Outreach Magazine* (Carlsbad, CA, 2012), p. 66.

## CHAPTER 3

1. Definitions for "Therismos: harvest" found in *Thayer's Greek Lexicon*, http://www.biblehub.com/greek/2326.htm

2. Andrew Murray, *The Collected Works and Sermons of Reverend Andrew Murray*: Kindle Edition (The Christian Miracle Foundation, 2011), location 16062.

## CHAPTER 4

1. "Scripture taken from *The New American Standard Bible Version;* Copyright 1960, 1962, 1963, 1968, 1971, 1972, 1973, 1975, 1977, 1995 by The Lockman Foundation, used by permission."

2. Definitions for "Deomai" found from *Strong's Concordance*, http://www.biblehub.com/greek/1189.htm

3. Andrew Murray, *The Collected Works and Sermons of Reverend Andrew Murray*: Kindle Edition (The Christian Miracle Foundation, 2011), location 16031.

4. Dick Eastman, *No Easy Road: Inspirational Thoughts on Prayer*. (Grand Rapids, MI: Baker Books, a Division of Baker Book House Company, 1971), p. 97-98.

5. Used by Permission, *The Circle Maker: Praying Circles Around Your Biggest Dreams and Greatest Fears*. Mark Batterson (Grand Rapids, MI: Zondervan, 2011), p.133.

6. Joseph M. Stowell, *Simply Jesus: Experiencing the One Your Heart Longs For*. (Sisters, Oregon: Multnomah Publishers Inc., 2002), p. 14-15.

7. Ibid., p. 15.

## SECTION TWO

1. http://www.goodreads.com/quotes/266309-all-god-s-giants-havebeen-weak-men-who-did-great, accessed June 1, 2015

## CHAPTER 5

1. Rick Weinberg, "94: Derek and Dad Finish Olympic 400 Together," ESPN. com, http://espn.go.com/espn/espn25/story?page=moments/94 (accessed September 22, 2014).

2. Ibid.

3. Eugene H. Peterson, *The Message: The New Testament in Contemporary English*. (Colorado Springs, CO: NavPress Publishing Group, 1993), p. 73.

4. Arthur Bennett, *The Valley of Vision: A Collection of Puritan Prayers & Devotions*. (Carlisle, PA: The Banner of Truth Trust, 1975, reprinted 1994), p. 177.

5. Oswald Chambers, *My Utmost For His Highest*. Uhrichsville, Ohio: Barbour Publishing, Inc., 1963), April 25th Devotional Entry.

6. Luis Palau and Tim Robnett, *Telling the Story: Evangelism for the Next Generation*. (Ventura, CA: Regal Books from Gospel Light, 2006), p. 130.

## CHAPTER 6

1. George Verwer, *The George Verwer Collection: The Revolution of Love*. (First Hodder and Stoughton/OM Pubishing, edition 1983, revised 1984, first published, The Revolution of Love, 1989), p. 81.

2. John Piper, *Amazing Grace in the Life of William Wilberforce*. (Wheaton, Illinois: Crossway Books, a Publishing Ministry of Good News Publishers, 2006), 32. Cited in Robert Isaac Wilberforce and Samuel Wilberforce, *The Life of William Wilberforce*, abridged edition (London, 1843), p. 48.

3. Ibid., p. 42. Cited from Pollock, "A Man Who Changed His Times," in *Character Counts: Leadership Qualities in Washington, Wilberforce, Lincoln, and Solzhenitsyn*, Ed. Os Guinness (Grand Rapids, Mich.: Baker House, 1999), p. 87.

4. Ibid., p. 42-43, Cited from John Pollock, *Wilberforce* (London: Constable and Company, 1977), 148 and 205 respectively.

5. Eric Metaxas, *How Then Should We Work: Furthering the Kingdom. From BreakPoint Commentaries*, October 25, 2012, reprinted with permission of Prison Fellowship,www.breakpoint.org.

## CHAPTER 7

1. Randy Alcorn, *The Treasure Principle: Discovering The Secret of Joyful Giving*. (Sisters, OR: Multnomah Publishers, Inc., 2001), p. 42-43.

2. Dick Eastman, *Beyond Imagination: A Simple Plan to Save the World.*(Grand Rapids, MI: Chosen Books, 1997), p. 283-284.

## CHAPTER 9

1. Steve Smith with Ying Kai, *T4T: A Discipleship Re-Revolution.* (Monument, CO: WIGTake Resources, 2011), p. 96-97.

2. George Verwer, *The George Verwer Collection: The Revolution of Love.* (First Hodder and Stoughton/OM Pubishing, edition 1983, revised 1984, first published, *The Revolution of Love*, 1989), p. 65-66.

3. Study Note on Mark 8:34 in *English Standard Version Study Bible;* Kindle Edition; Crossway Bibles, 2008, USA. (Cross-reference verses have been removed to help the flow of the read, but it appears in the notes).

4. Nancy Leigh DeMoss, *Brokenness: The Heart God Revives.* (Chicago, IL: Moody Publishers, 2002) p. 111-112.

5. Material provided by the *Voice of the Martyrs,*PO Box 443, Bartlesville, OK 74003. 1-918-337-8015. For more information, see www.persecution. com. Email: thevoice@vom-usa.org. (July 1999)

## EPILOGUE

1. http://www.spurgeongems.org/vols19-21/chs1127.pdf

In January of 2006, P. J. Meduri Ministries was formed. The ministry, now known as Taking the Field Ministries, is an international evangelistic association that focuses on large and small outreach initiatives, training in relational evangelism, and schools of evangelism and discipleship. The ministry is a 501 (c) (3) tax-exempt organization governed by a Board of Directors. If anyone is interested in having P. J. speak in your area or church, help with community outreaches, or provide training in relational evangelism, please contact him at one of the following:

**TAKING THE FIELD MINISTRIES**

**P. J. Meduri**
**Director**

**440.708.3675**

**www.takingthefield.org**
**pj@takingthefield.org**

MEMBER
**NEXT GENERATION ALLIANCE**
A MINISTRY OF THE LUIS PALAU ASSOCIATION

*..So that My Salvation may reach*
*to the end of the earth. (Isa. 49:6)*

**Box 961**
**Kent, OH 44240**

**&**

**Box 433**
**Glen Daniel, WV 25844**